THE COMPLETE WHIPPET

The Complete
WHIPPET

by Louis Pegram

First Edition/Third Printing

1982
HOWELL BOOK HOUSE Inc.
230 Park Avenue
New York, N. Y. 10169

Contents

*Drawings, pp. 1, 4, 16, 32, 61, 90, 156 and 217 are by Donna
Bangs. Drawings in Chapter 10 are by Mary Beth Arthur.*

About the Author

Louis PEGRAM may well be considered the Dean of American Whippetdom. His credentials as a successful breeder, show exhibitor, sponsor and participant in racing are impeccable. His contributions to the breed as its leading historian, writer, commentator and club official certainly qualify him for that illustrious title.

Louis has worked extensively in all phases of purebred dogs since childhood. His father, Dr. L. J. Pegram, was the first all-breed judge from North Carolina and served as president of the first all-breed show-giving club in that state, the Carolina Kennel Club in Albany.

He has actively bred, owned, raced and handled several breeds with special emphasis on Whippets, Greyhounds, Wire Fox Terriers and pointing dogs. His dogs have won Bests of Breed and group placements at many well-known shows in America including those of the Westminster Kennel Club, Morris & Essex Kennel Club, Maryland Kennel Club and the Kennel Club of Philadelphia. Pegram-owned Greyhounds have raced successfully at most of the major tracks in America. From 1948 to 1959, Mr. Pegram maintained a kennel averaging 100 Greyhounds annually. Currently, the Pegram kennel contains from 12 to 25 Whippets for breeding, show and race purposes.

Serving on the Board of Directors of the American Whippet Club for seventeen years, he is now its president. He has written the monthly breed column in *Pure-bred Dogs—American Kennel Gazette* for several years.

Louis Pegram

His vocation in dog nutrition dates back to 1944 when he joined the Ralston Purina Company in charge of all pet foods sold along the East Coast and Canada. From 1952 to 1959 he served with the Gaines Division of General Foods Corporation in Kankakee, Illinois and Battle Creek, Michigan as National Manager of Professional Sales. Since 1960 he has been Director of Professional Services at Ralston Purina.

It would be difficult to find his peer as an authority in the annals of Whippetry. Into *The Complete Whippet* Mr. Pegram has poured his incomparable research, knowledge, experience and love for the breed. This first hardbound book on the breed published in America presents all the fascinating facets of this multi-purpose dog, from its early origins to its present functions as a companion, show, obedience, and racing paragon.

For a personal note as the publisher, may I add that my own purebred dog interest has spanned several decades with close exposure to some two-dozen breeds. And, as the happy owner of a Whippet for the past three years, I have found that no breed surpasses it in its combined attributes of versatility, intelligence, beauty, cleanliness, ease of care, adaptability, docility, devotion and—the sheer joys of its ownership.

It is my fervent wish that Mr. Pegram's dedicated work herein will educate and inspire other dog lovers to share the joys and rewards of Whippet ownership.

—*Elsworth Howell,* publisher

The Whippet is the picture of classic, canine beauty. Whether standing still or on the move, the Whippet is one of the most esthetically-pleasing dog breeds.

Introduction

THE VERSATILITY of the Whippet as a breed has been a great inspiration to me since childhood. My life with Whippets has been a full one, but not all stages have been fun and success. Personally, I have known over three-fourths of the Whippets and their owners mentioned in the pages of this book. Of greater personal importance, it has been my lifelong pleasure to participate in the breeding, showing, racing and coursing of this wonderful, little canine athlete, who in most cases is also a superior pet, friend and house dog.

There is no one person to whom this book is dedicated. Special thanks should go to the many friends of the breed who furnished photographs and background information that so greatly helped in making possible the history of the Whippet. Major contributors are the ladies of the Clerical Service Department of Ralston Purina Company who, in their spare time, typed all copy.

It has been time-consuming, often frustrating, but a great pleasure to document this history of our breed. Whole books could be written on the contributions of dedicated owners and their outstanding Whippets of the past and present. The same is true of information on breeding, care and training. The background of the Whippet is that multifaceted.

Hopefully, *The Complete Whippet* will inform many interested people of the numerous merits of this versatile breed and make the interesting details of his history available to all.

The Kershaw children, Selina, Herbert and Evelyn with their Whippet, Cutaway. This photograph was taken in England around 1895.

1

Development
of the Breed

───────────────────────────────

BREED history can be fascinating and challenging reading to owners interested in learning more about their breed. Unprovable history can have great fictional value, but facts can be greatly affected by the opinions and writing style of an author. It is hoped that the material covered here on the early development of the Whippet in England and America will be of value and interest to the reader. Every effort has been made to present fact and/or true logic, based on the rich heritage of the Whippet—a balanced combination of ideal pet, elegant show animal and racing dog of rare ability.

Early Origins

There are some unprovable opinions on the early origin of the breed, as well as the true meaning of the word Whippet. It is entirely possible the breed name originally related to a small, short-coated type of all-purpose pet dog. The accents in various districts of England could easily explain early references to the words "Whippert" or "Whoppet." It should be remembered that several centuries ago few people were well-educated, written records were virtually nonexistent, and communications and travel were difficult at best. There was no protection for dogs against distemper, little was known about parasite control, mange, and other complaints. Even less was known about nutrition, resulting in common incidence of rickets, black tongue, and other deficiency diseases. Few dogs, regardless of breed or ownership, reached maturity.

By the mid-1800s information relating to facts indicated that in the heavily industrial areas of Northern England, there existed a small breed of dogs that resembled a Greyhound, in miniature and often showed strong traces of Terrier, Italian Greyhound or characteristics of other breeds. These small dogs were called Whippets and were noted for their ability as silent hunters of small game. In some areas Whippet races were held for amusement on non-working days. These little Greyhound-like dogs were raced over a level surface such as fields, meadows and streets of the smaller towns. The owners, mainly working men, took great pride in the racing ability of their Whippets. So great was the popularity of *rag racing* on a straight course, where a Whippet ran from one man to his owner some 200 yards away, that the breed soon acquired the nickname "the poor man's race horse." Arguments were many and varied based on claims of incorrect weights, incorrect handling of Whippets at the start and walking up on the racers before the finish of a race. Flaming tempers, sharp tongues and swinging fists often were a part of the afternoon's entertainment at the Whippet races. As rag racing grew in popularity among the lower income groups, interest in the Whippet as a *snap dog* used for silent hunting and killing rabbits in a closed area declined.

Stabilizing Type in the Whippet

The development of the Whippet as a breed is not glamorous. All Whippets did not result from exactly the same crosses of other breeds with the Greyhound. Whippets used for hunting and racing were heavy in Terrier blood to give added strength and desire. Whippets used strictly as pets or for ornamental purposes generally showed more strongly the influence of the Italian Greyhound, used to reduce size and give greater refinement. The many crosses with Greyhound-type individuals to establish the Whippet as a breed, explains why today's Whippet is such a sturdy, healthy breed with few health and heredity problems. By the late 1800s a Whippet-type sighthound had been established, and Whippet-type was bred to Whippet-type for uniformity in appearance. This kind of breeding program continued until the Whippet was accepted by the Kennel Club (England) and the American Kennel Club (U.S.A.) as eligible for registration.

14

The Lurcher

The Lurcher, a crossbred Greyhound, should not be confused with the Whippet. Hunting dogs of many types and breeds were used by the wealthy and poor alike to hunt and/or catch game. A Lurcher is a cross of any purebred or mongrel with a Greyhound. The poor, generally poachers and gypsies, preferred a fast hunter that did not bark and would run down its prey. The wealthy and middle-class land-owning gentry would often cross the Greyhound with Pointers, Setters, Spaniels and Retrievers to get an all-purpose hunting dog. In cases of this type, Lurchers were used for flushing or indicating the location of game.

Breeding Whippets to Greyhounds still is reasonably popular in Northern England for racing purposes. This type of cross is a blending of two similar types or strains with the difference being mostly a matter of size. The result of crossing a Whippet to a Greyhound has been considered a Lurcher by the English since the Whippet became recognized by the Kennel Club.

The Sporting Whippet

The Whippet originally enjoyed its greatest popularity with the working classes of Northern England. When the Whippet became more popular around London, there was great division in thinking among the middle-income group and the laboring men of the industrial North. Royalty was occasionally mentioned, but in reality it was the middle-class that devoted its attention to the show ring, and largely the lower income group to racing, coursing and hunting of small game. Lack of communications between the groups and the split in interest between show and racing was primarily the reason for racing Whippets in England being graded by weight, while show Whippets were measured for height at the highest point of the shoulder blades (withers). Many Whippet fanciers interested only in showing did not think it "nice" to even mention the word Whippet, as it related to a race dog.

Breed Recognition

The first real efforts to recognize the Whippet as a registerable breed started when Mr. Herbert Viccars requested acceptance to The Stud Book in 1890, and in 1891 the Whippet was recognized by the Kennel Club in England. It was not until 1899, largely through the efforts of Mr. E. T. Cox, that the Whippet Club, parent club of the breed, was formed, primarily to promote a Standard of the breed. This Club was interested in the Whippet as a show dog, and had little or no interest in racing. Among these pioneers were F. H. Bottomley, Manorley Kennels, and Albert Lamotte, Shirley Kennels. Many of the outstanding show Whippets can be traced to Ch. Shirley Wanderer and his son, Ch. Manorley Maroni. These two outstanding sires could well be considered the pillars of the breed, both in England and in the United States.

The American Kennel Club registered its first Whippet in 1888. The dog was Jack Dempsey, No. 9804, born September 23, 1885. Owned by Charles O. Breed, Lynn, Massachusetts and bred by P. H. Hoffman, Philadelphia, Pennsylvania. From his whelping date, he could not have been named after the famous heavy-weight champion who reigned from 1919 to 1926.

In spite of the fact that the American Kennel Club registered its first Whippet three years before the breed was recognized by the governing body in its native country, interest in the Whippet and activities in its behalf were not strong until after World War I. It was the Whippet's double-suitability as a show dog and racer and the affluence of the day that began to project the Whippet's star in the American dog fancy.

2

The Whippet During the 1920s

INTEREST and Whippet population in America was very limited until after World War I. The breed was now recognized by the American Kennel Club and the Kennel Club of England. Requirements to register dogs with both organizations were very flexible, and many Whippet owners did not see the value of registration papers. Many owners felt that registration papers recorded with an official registration bureau were no better than the honesty of the breeder filling out the pedigree. Owners felt that their word was sufficient and the handling of papers by a registration bureau was just an extra expense. Very few of the racing Whippets in Northern England were registered with the Kennel Club, but most owners knew the breeding of their dogs. The Whippet Club, England, did an outstanding job of insisting that all of their members own only dogs registered with the Kennel Club. Members of The Whippet Club were interested largely in the breed as a dog and pet. This club functioned on a very limited basis during World War I, but became very active immediately after the war.

This scene from a 1920s West Coast race meeting shows handlers and their dogs heading for the starting line. The gentleman on the right is James Young and he is carrying a rough-coated Whippet of the type frequently seen on the race course at that time. *Photo courtesy Christine Cormany.*

American Beginnings

The Whippet came to America in the 1920s as an extremely respected breed. A few Whippets found their way to the New World as part of the possessions of immigrants from Northern England. The great majority, however, were imported at high prices by wealthy sportsmen typical of the era. There should be absolutely no doubt that the most desirable Whippets were considered race dogs. Premium prices were paid for combination race and show Whippets that were registered by the Kennel Club or the American Kennel Club. The two clubs honored each other's registrations and papers could be easily transferred from one organization to the other. Many dogs were imported for both show and racing with the seller's written word being the only record of registration. This policy of honoring the seller's word, with no official registration papers was soon to become a major problem for those who wished permanent records of parentage on dogs used for breeding, racing and shows. Only 28 Whippets were registered by the American Kennel Club in 1926 showing the seriousness of the situation.

The glamorous, lusty years during the prohibition era following World War I, often referred to as the roaring 20s, put new life in the Whippet as a breed in America. It was during the period of 1924 through 1929 that the Whippet first became known as complete based upon race, show and pet qualities. Many of the policies followed today under official rules and regulations for national Whippet racing, as approved by the American Whippet Club, had their start in the late 1920s.

Early Fanciers and Dogs

Much of the credit for promoting the Whippet with emphasis on racing should go to Freeman A. Ford, Arroyo Kennels, Pasadena, California; Felix Angus Leser, Freemanor Kennel, Stevenson, Maryland; Harry E. Damon, Jr., Short Hills, New Jersey; Mae Bland, Columbus, Ohio; Blanch S. Harring, Sparrows Point, Maryland; James F. Young, Calgary, and Pasadena, California; William J. Kelly, Maryland and Frank Tuffley, Kinsman Kennels, Cleveland, Ohio. Other active owner/breeders of the period were William S. Short, Poconosique Kennels, Middletown, New York; J. Bailey Wilson, Media, Pennsylvania; Arthur Rankin, Hollywood, California; Elsa H. Voss, Westbury, New York; Amy L. Bonham, York, Pennsylvania; McClure Halley, Brooklyn, New York; Bayard Tuckerman, Boston, Massachusetts; William Anderson Coull, Portland, Oregon; Joseph P. Day, New York, New York; Helen P. Rosemont, San Francisco, California; Marion Woodcock, San Gabriel, California;

19

Blanche T. Steers, Washington, D.C.; George S. West, Chestnut Hill, Massachussetts; Mrs. Hadley, Tatiana Kennels, Erie, Pennsylvania; Mrs. C. Shuttleworth, N. Hollywood, California; Ben F. Lewis, Lansdowne, Pennsylvania; Mrs. Charles G. West, Jr., Westbury, New York; Howard Stout Neilson, Darien, Connecticut and James Harriess, Steubenville, Ohio.

Whippets of this period could be recognized as such but were lacking in elegance, size and soundness as compared to those of the 1970s. Average weight for combined sexes was 17 pounds. Most Whippets had short muzzles. Some had very strong bites, indicating a Terrier heritage while others had narrow muzzles, lacking strength of bite. Feet were poor in the majority of cases, often with very long toes and weak pasterns. Many ears pointed skyward (gay). Coats varied from very thick skin with little hair to heavy, woolly undercoats with many showing rough, bristly guard hairs. Some were short and blocky with great balance and determination. Those preferred for show were small, leggy and delicate. Some truly resembled a large, long-legged mouse with their delicate pointed heads, long, finger-like toes and thin skin.

Whippet owners were very careful to keep extended 3- to 5-generation pedigrees on most dogs used for breeding show and racing when information was available. Some pedigrees were not complete, but all known parentage was listed when possible. Most pedigrees were kept up to date, even though many of the Whippets were not registered. Most dogs had short one or two-word names, such as Luce, Enid, Martha, Timid Tim, White Legs, Little Wack, etc. A few of the larger breeders used kennel names, e.g., Freemanor, Arroyo, Nomad, Manorley, Shirley or Bland's. But all names were short ones.

In the late 1920s some champions and known producers of quality were heavily line bred. This close line breeding probably reflects the small number of top-quality Whippets available for breeding at the time. Many breeders of livestock and poultry relied heavily on in-breeding and line breeding to intensify desired qualities. When this type of close-relation family breeding is handled properly, it can produce great individuals.

The Whippets found most often in both outcross and line bred pedigrees were Student, Ch. Black Prince, Ch. Willesbeaux, Ch. Taffy's Pride, Ch. Strathcona King and the fine brood bitch, Int. Ch. Nomad Nancy of Oxon. It should be noted that five of these six great producing Whippets were not from the same or closely related families, reflecting great ability to reproduce as individuals.

Other outstanding winning and producing Whippets of the 1920s were Int. Ch. Freemanor Galloping Dominoes, Int. Ch. Freemanor Glencoe Supreme, Ch. Arroyo Rhoda, Ch. Arroyo Strathcona Girl, Ch. Broadway Granite Oak Masterpiece, Ch. Broadway Granite Oak Molly, Ch. Broadway Admiration, Ch. Freemanor Galloping Ghost, Ch. Erin Torpedo, Ch.

```
                              Ch. Manorley Maori
              Ch. Manorley Merman
                              Luce
STUDENT (male)
                              Ch. Manorley Maori
              Ch. Waford Glory
                              Shirley Pride




                                    Sir Joseph
                       Devonshire Lad
                                    Maggie
CH. BLACK PRINCE (male)
                                    Cripple
                       Barberryhill Nip
                                    Beauty




                                    Willesbea
                       Ch. Willesbeaux
                                    Winstar
CH. NOMAD NANCY OF OXON
       (female)
                                    Spring Morn
                       Lark's Song
                                    Enid
```

```
                                  Searchlight
                   Ch. Willcsbea
                                  Spray
CH. WILLESBEAUX (male)
                                  Ch. Shirley Sunstar
                   Winstar
                                  Falside Fascination




                                  Better Luck
                   Watford Bon
                                  Ch. Kemmel
CH. TAFFY'S PRIDE (male)
                                  Towyside Smoke
                   Girl Guide
                                  Ch. Carnation




                                  Shirley Dandy
                   Sunstar
                                  Tiba
CH. STRATHCONA KING (male)
                                  Young Tittlemouse
                   Sunbright
                                  Red Rose
```

22

Arroyo Big Hearted Bye, Ch. Arroyo Probably Not, Ch. Bland's Pacemaker, Ch. Bland's Pathfinder, Ch. Percy of Oxon, Ch. Coolridge Sunshower, Ch. Blue Pilot of Tatiania.

Both registered and unregistered purebred dogs could be shown, even when full knowledge of pedigree was unknown. An unregistered purebred dog could be shown as *listed* for a small additional fee. Catalogs varied greatly in listing breeds, classes, prizes, etc. Sales price was often listed beside a dog's name in the catalog. Most major shows gave only awards of Best Male and Best Female; there was seldom a Best of Breed award. Six Whippets shown gave five points toward a bench championship to the winner.

Racing During the 1920s

Four men deserve much of the credit for handling the physical side of putting on race meetings: William J. Kelly and Jack Davies in the East, Frank Tuffley in the Midwest and Jim Young in California. William Kelly, born in Keighley, Yorkshire, England, is still alive at this writing and active in purebred dogs. Bill, or Willie as he is known to his friends, came to America at 23 years of age having trained racing pigeons and Whippets in England. Soon after arrival in America young Kelly joined with Terrier handler Jack Davies of Linden, New Jersey in training racing Whippets at Wissahickon Farms near Philadelphia. The Kelly-Davies combination then took 84 Whippets to Bermuda for three months of exhibition racing. Upon returning to the United States, this combination furnished racing Whippets and track equipment for daily race meetings along the East coast but concentrated much of their effort around Baltimore, Philadelphia, and the Long Island area. The daily charge for dogs and equipment was from $200.00 to $300.00. Generally a series of races would be run in the afternoon and another series in the evening.

James Young started with Whippets in 1906 and remained active in the breed until his death in the late 1960s. In 1924 his great love for Whippet racing caused him to resign from the Canadian-Pacific Railway, taking over the management of the fine Arroyo Kennels owned by Mr. Freeman A. Ford. Arroyo Kennels, under the guidance of James Young, was the most active breeder of rough-coated Whippets in America. These little dogs were outstanding racers and were campaigned heavily along the West Coast. Several were sent East and established outstanding race records. Jim Young was the heart of Whippet racing in Southern California until the depression of the 1930s which made it necessary for the Arroyo Kennels to discontinue operation. Jim Young's greatest contribution to Whippets in America was a daughter now known as Christine Cormany who has carried on in the footsteps of her father.

During the 1920s Whippets were hand-slipped at the start of a race. The heaviest dog in a race started from scratch while lighter contestants were given yards advantage based on their weight.   *Photo courtesy Christine Cormany.*

Early Whippet racing in America featured separate lanes three feet wide and 16″ off the ground for each contestant. A dog was disqualified if he left his lane during the running of a race.   *Photo courtesy Christine Cormany.*

Frank Tuffley confined his racing and show efforts mostly to the State of Ohio. Frank was dedicated to Whippet racing and was active in holding race meetings until his death in the mid-1960s. Frank Tuffley loved rag racing, but was very slow to change to more modern racing methods.

The greatest showcase of quality for the Whippet as a combination race and show dog was the National Whippet Derby under the auspices of the Whippet Club of America. The race meeting was held at American League Ballpark, Washington, D.C., May 20 and 21, 1927. Officers were Mr. Charles G. Hopton, America's most respected all-breed judge; Manager and Head Referee, Mr. Harry Damon, Jr., Secretary of the Whippet Club of America; Clerk of Course and Mr. Emory A. Stone, starter; Mr. Felix Angus Leser, handicapper. Patrons and patronesses included very large numbers of politicians and social figures of the United States and Europe. Included in the list was the Secretary of War, Secretary of Agriculture, Speaker of the House of Representatives and Ambassadors from six nations including England, Ireland and Italy.

The three major races were the International Handicap with a purse of $400.00 and trophies, Debutante Handicap, $300.00 plus trophies, American- and Canadian-Bred Handicap with purse of $200.00 and trophies and the Consolation Handicap with $300.00 and a trophy presented by Mary Roberts Rinehart. Whippets taking part in the National Derby came from every section of America where racing was held.

A special race was held for the great show and race bitch, Ch. Nomad Nancy of Oxon, who raced against her litter; Champions Nomad's Sister Sue, Sammy, Zev, Epinard, My Own and Papyrus. Mr. Percy Roberts, one of our most popular all-breed judges, was also interested in early racing in the U.S.A. Percy felt that Nancy of Oxon was the best bitch of her time.

Most Whippet tracks acceptable for rag racing were generally 200 yards long with an allowance of 20-30 yards for stopping the dogs at the end of the race. The track is divided into four or six lanes 3-4 feet wide and separated by a heavy cloth tape or rope held up by pegs 10-16 inches from the ground. Each Whippet runs in his own separate lane and is disqualified if he jumps from the lane at any point in a race. It requires two people to race a Whippet in rag racing just as is true in training a Whippet for racing today. The person holding the dog at the start of the race is called the handler, holder, slipper or chucker. At the start of a race the holder stands in the center of the lane with one foot on the line marking the weight advantage given his Whippet. He quickly releases the dog when the starting pistol is fired in the air. The holder can release the dog or throw or pitch him in stride. A good holder can often steal five to eight lengths if his racer has been properly trained for a fast-breaking start. Before the race gets under way, the owner or catcher of the Whippet, at the end of the track, runs down the track past the finish staying in his dog's

This scene (circa 1925) shows one of the first Whippet races held on the Mid-wick Polo Field. Note the owners behind the finish line waving towels at their dogs after the English fashion of rag racing.

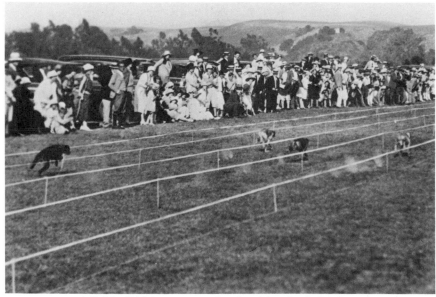

A field of Whippets pressing hard for the finish line.
Photo courtesy Christine Cormany.

A partial view of the main runs of Freeman Ford's Arroyo Kennels. From its base of operations in Pasadena, California, Arroyo sent dogs to shows and race meetings far and wide, garnering many honors in both.

James Young, kennel manager for Arroyo, with a group of the kennel's show and racing competitors.

27

Arroyo Kennels was known for both rough and smooth-coated Whippets during its period of activity. Here is one of the kennel's rough-coated race Whippets with James Young.

Jack Davies (left) and William Kelley, photographed following their return from Bermuda.

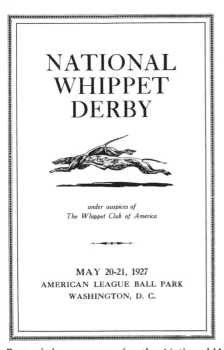

NATIONAL
WHIPPET
DERBY

under auspices of
The Whippet Club of America

MAY 20-21, 1927
AMERICAN LEAGUE BALL PARK
WASHINGTON, D. C.

ENTRIES

INTERNATIONAL HANDICAP

Sloe Eyes—Dunlap Castle
Arroyo Benjarry—Freeman A. Ford
Arroyo What Not—Freeman A. Ford
Polly—William Yates, Arlington, N.J.
Tanguay — Glenn O'Roak, Boston, Mass.
Sarah Porter—Dunlap Castle, Hollywood, Cal.
Nylgha—Stuart Edington, Keyser, W. Va.
Ghurka—F. R. Edington, Boston, Mass.
Coomassie—James Gilligan, Lawrence, Mass.
Orphan Girl—Sidney R. Rollins, Mattapan, Mass.

Barberryhill Margaret—Bayard Warren, Prides Crossing, Mass.
Lion—P. A. and J. B. Draper, Boston, Mass.
Cinders—P. A. and J. B. Draper, Boston, Mass.
Blue Smoke—P. A. and J. B. Draper, Boston, Mass.
Telleau—Joseph Draper, Boston, Mass.
Red Rose—G. A. Porter, Bentonville, Ark.
Dew Drop—A. E. Bland, Columbus, Ohio
Wild Rose—A. E. Bland, Columbus, Ohio
On Time—A. E. Bland, Columbus, Ohio

AMERICAN AND CANADIAN BRED

Sarah Porter—Dunlap Castle, Hollywood, Cal.
Flying Scotchman—Mary Pool, Abington, Mass.
Freemanor Galloping Ghost—Mrs. B. H. Haring, Sparrows Point, Md
Atalanta—Mrs. Richard Goodwin, Garden City, N. Y.
Dew Drop, A. E. Bland, Columbus, Ohio
Wild Rose—A. E. Bland, Columbus, Ohio
On Time—A. E. Bland, Columbus, Ohio
Fargo Sam—A. E. Bland, Columbus, Ohio

Blue Boy—A. M. Wills, N. J.
Mischievous—W. Coombs, N. J.
Cyclone—Harry Lindsay, N. J.
Little Lida—Harry Lindsay, N. J.
Darkie—R. MacLusky, East Orange, N. J.
Nomad Black Jack—Jack Davies, Linden, N. J.
To Go—R. MacLusky, East Orange, N. J.
Full Speed—Dorothy E. Greene, Washington, D. C.
Free Silver, Elizabeth Engle, Washington, D. C.
First Say—Jack Davies, Linden, N. J.

DEBUTANTE HANDICAP

Dew Drop—A. E. Bland, Columbus, Ohio
Bobbie Ann—Mrs. E. J. Whitall, Washington, D. C.
Fargo Sam—A. E. Bland, Columbus, Ohio
Step Lively—A. E. Bland, Columbus, Ohio
June—Joseph P. Draper, Boston, Mass.
Maggie—William Yates, Arlington, N. J.
Freemanor Dazzle—Mrs. B. H. Haring, Sparrows Point, Md.
To Go—Rupert H. MacLusky, East Orange, N. J.
Flying Scotchman—Mary Pool, Abington, Mass.
Abington Futurity—Mrs. James Pool, Abington, Mass.

Pretty Polly—M. Dunleavy, New York City.
Northern Light — Bayard Warren, Prides Crossing, Mass.
Wriggles—J. Moffet, N. J.
Five Spot—P. Summerfield, N. J.
Film Star—Jack Davies, Linden, N. J.
Nomad Nancy of Oxon—Harry E. Damon, Jr., Short Hills, N. Y.
Nomad Zev—Mrs. Sydney A. Beggs, Short Hills, N. J.
Nomad Sammy—Mrs. Sydney A. Beggs, Short Hills, N. J.
Nomad My Own—Thyrza Steers, Washington, D. C.
Nomad Epinard—Laura Day, Short Hills, N. J.
Nomad Sister Sue—Harry E. Damon, Jr., Short Hills, N. J.

7

Part of the program for the National Whippet Derby held during 1927 in Washington, D.C. This important affair for the breed and for racing is fully discussed in the text.

Puget Sound Kennel Club, Inc.

FIRST ANNUAL
NORTHWEST WHIPPET RACES
At
University of Washington Stadium, Seattle

JULY 17, 1926

By Sanction of American Kennel Club and Under Racing Rules of Whippet Club of America

FIRST HEAT AT 2:00 P. M.

Officials

CAPT. CHARLES TENNANT..............President
WM. GYLDENFELDT..............Vice-President
JOHN H. PRESTON..............Secretary-Treasurer

EXECUTIVE COMMITTEE
CAPT. TENNANT
WM. GYLDENFELDT
CHARLES H. HOWELL
DR. L. W. BRYDON

JUDGES
CAPT. TENNANT
WM. GYLDENFELDT
D. E. ("TUBBY") GRAVES

REFEREE
A. E. GRAFTON

CLERK OF COURSE
GERALD L. STOCK

TIMEKEEPER
RAY SHELDON

RACE STEWARD
WM. H. PYM

CLERK OF SCALES
ROBERT MUNRO

HANDICAPPER
ROBERT MUNRO

ANNOUNCER
DICK STOCKWELL

MARKSMEN
W. J. EVANS
SANDY MACLEAN

PUBLICITY MANAGER
HAL S. NELSON

SECRETARY-MANAGER
JOHN H. PRESTON

Fairborne Kennels, Route 4, Box 147, Olympia, Wash.

Part of the program for the first Northwest Whippet races.

Premium List
of the
Vancouver and District Whippet Association.
C. K. C. RULES

VANCOUVER EXHIBITION GROUNDS
May 24th, 1927

Executive Officers:
W. T. OATES..............President
JOE KERR..............Vice-President

Bench Show Committee:
GERALD L. STOCK
W. T. CLIFT
W A COULL
C. W. WALKER
W. THOMSON
W. H. PYM (Chairman)

Veterinary Surgeon
DR. W. J. BALLARD

Specialty Judge:
J. A. MEADOWS, Vancouver, B. C.

Ring Stewards:
CHAS. M. WALKER
WILLIAM CLIFT

Superintendent:
JOE KERR

Secretary-Treasurer:
H. J. DUNN
1365 Howe Street, Vancouver, B. C.; Douglas 3707 R

SHOW RULES

1. No dog will be received after 10 a.m., May 24th. Judging of dogs will commence at 11 a.m. and will continue at intervals.
2. The Bench Show Committee will use intelligence for the care and safety of all dogs exhibited.
3. No dog will be received unless supplied with a suitable collar and chain. A swivel chain is much the safer.
4. The Superintendent will have full charge of the show.
5. Entries must be made on blanks furnished by the Secretary.
6. An entrance fee of $1.00 will be charged for the first entry of a dog; 75 cents for the second entry and 50 cents for the following entries of the same dog.
7. Dogs not registered in the C. K. C. will, according to C. K. C. rules, be charged 25 cents listing fees.
8. The Committee reserves to themselves the right to refuse any entry that they may think fit to exclude.
9. The Show will open at 10 a.m.
10. During the hours of judging all dogs must remain in the building. If any dog is not found on its bench when called for by the Superintendent, the judging will proceed without it. In the absence of the owner, attendants will take the dog into the ring.
11. All dogs must be benched and not kept in crates during the Show.
12. No dogs will be allowed in the building unless entered.
13. Exhibitors may send their dogs by express upon prepayment of the Express Company's rates. Crates must be addressed in the name of the exhibitor in care of the Superintendent.

Premium list of the Vancouver and District Whippet Association.

lane, calling the dog and waving the cloth or rag to attract the Whippet's attention. Owners call their Whippets during the running of a race, but must stay at least thirty feet past the finish line to allow all Whippets to cross the finish line without interference.

Arguments were many based on supposed inaccurate weighing of Whippets, improper slipping at the start and walking up on the dogs at the finish line. It was all good fun but often not friendly fun.

Whippets in major races weighed from ten to 28 pounds, and were handicapped in races based on weight. There were many different types of weight handicap systems, none of which had any real accuracy in determining the true speed of the individual dog. Some systems gave the male one pound advantage over a female of the same weight. This method was later reversed to say both sexes of the same weight should have the same yard advantage. Probably the most acceptable weight handicap system used in the 1920s was starting the heaviest Whippets, 28 pounds, at the 200 yard mark known as scratch (X). Each Whippet less than 28 pounds received a one yard starting advantage, per pound from 28 pounds down to 17 pounds. Whippets from 17 pounds to 10 pounds received a two yard per pound weight advantage, e.g., a Whippet who weighed 26 pounds ran only 198 yards, 23 pounds 195 yards, etc. (Weight and sex are not the determining factor in speed.) A good, heavyweight Whippet will generally outrun a good lightweight Whippet. A slow Whippet in the 20-28 pound category will often be defeated by a superior racer in the 15-20 pound weight category without the use of the weight/yardage allowance. Very few Whippets under 15 pounds have the overall speed and the needed extra burst of speed to win over Whippets in the heavier weight categories.

The national economy and all types of entertainment were booming as we entered the year 1928. Whippet racing was no exception. So great was the interest in the sport that the first permanent Whippet track was built on the property in back of The Valley Inn, Brooklandville, Maryland. This was a 230-yard straight track with sand and clay footing, grandstand and a permanent kennel for housing Whippets on a monthly basis. The compact little plant could handle about 1,000 spectators and operated at first on Saturday and Sunday afternoons but later switched to night racing on other than Sundays. Costs of construction and maintenance of the track came from a portion of the income through bookmakers, admission, programs, food and soft drinks. There was no purse money for Whippet owners at this time. Expenses were high in operating a track of this type.

The Valley Inn was the best known gathering place in the famous sporting area known as Green Spring Valley. Many of the most prominent sportsmen and social figures found this one of their favorite spots for socializing. If you wanted good food and a piece of the action in Maryland, this was the place. Those who were largely responsible for the first suc-

An interest in Whippets can be a long-term affair. This photo, taken in 1922, shows Mrs. James M. Austin with the West sisters, Betty and Barbara. Betty (left) is now Mrs. Philip S. P. Fell.

The daughter of James Young inherited her father's enthusiasm for Whippets. Today she is known to all as Christine Cormany.

cessful permanent Whippet track in America were Felix Angus Leser, Evans Bramble, Charles Brawner, Homer B. Kahn, Herman Ducker and Captain John Hatfield, owner of The Valley Inn. William Kelly was full-time, salaried kennel master and had charge of all racing Whippets. This group operated as the Whippet Club which soon took on the name of the Maryland Whippet Club.

The stock market crashed in 1929 and so did the economy of America. The booming economy of the 20s was over, and the roaring 20s roared no more.

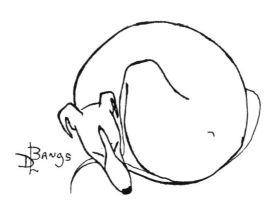

3

The Whippet: 1930-1955

T HE STOCK Market crash of 1929, followed by the Depression years of the thirties, hit Whippet activities in America like an atomic bomb. Most of the wealthy sporting patrons, who were largely responsible for the financial support and backed most Whippet activities in America, quickly withdrew from the hobby. Only the permanent Whippet track at Brooklandville, Maryland weathered the financial storm and actually grew stronger both in attendance and new Whippet ownership. Dog shows during this period were few in America, most being held in major cities with large populations. Entries at most all-breed shows were still small reflecting the Whippet population in America. All-breed dog shows held in the areas where Whippet racing existed drew by far the largest breed entries, clearly indicating many owners of this period were interested both in racing and showing.

The Meander Influence

The year 1930 marked the start of Meander Kennels, located at Locust Dale, Virginia. This kennel, owned by Miss F. Julia and Miss Judith R. Shearer, dominated Whippet breeding in America for twenty years and was still a major factor in the breeding and showing of Whippets until the death of both sisters early in the 1970s. The first Whippet owned by Judith Shearer was Milk of Magnesia by Ch. Peter of Oxon out of Fascination, bred by E. Coe Kerr.

Ch. Sandbrilliant of Meander, an English import and the foundation stud dog of the Shearer sisters' celebrated Meander kennels.

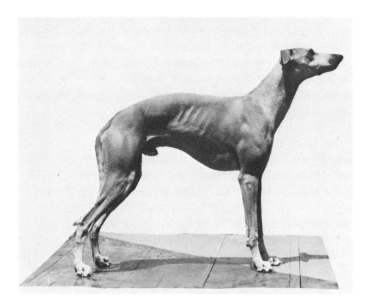

Ch. Mica of Meander, owned and bred by Meander Kennels, was considered by many the best show dog and stud bred by the Shearers. He was the first Whippet to draw the attention of Group judges to the breed.

Much of the early success of Meander was based on the mating of Ch. Sandbrilliant of Meander to Ch. Syndicate. This breeding was repeated several times and produced 15 champions, plus numerous other get, who were successful on the race track, but did not finish their show championships. Offspring of Ch. Sandbrilliant and Ch. Syndicate crossed well with virtually all families of Whippets of that period. Ch. Mica and Ch. Slag were considered the best males from this mating, both in the show ring and for siring quality offspring. Two of the more successful early Meander matings were Ch. Mica of Meander to Tiptree Sheila and San Benito Flash. Ch. Thelma of Meander, a sister to Ch. Mica, was mated twice to Ch. Sept of Althea, producing the outstanding show and circular track racers, Ch. Pegram's Red Wagon and Ch. Clansman of Ups and Downs. Both of these Whippets went on to produce high quality show and race individuals. The success of Meander Whippets in the 1930s completely changed the appearance of many show and racing dogs. A definite type was established, and the vast majority of Meander-bred Whippets could be easily identified by knowledgeable fanciers as "Meander type." Most were solid yellow, red or fawn with dark hazel eyes, often with a few black hairs throughout the body and some had black muzzles. The Althea and Tiptree bloodlines often brought white into certain of the early families of Meander Whippets, but did not greatly change their uniformity and type. Both Julia and Judy Shearer preferred solid-colored Whippets with dark eyes. So great was the impact of Meander type during the 1930s and 1940s, that many Whippet owners called them the "American type." Most Meander Whippets were true English-type Greyhounds in miniature covering much ground with a moderate, well-muscled arch over the loin. Heads were typically Greyhound in appearance with great length of muzzle and strength of bite. Feet were well-knuckled and good length of leg, strong pasterns, and rear angulation giving the appearance of strength and drive. Virtually all had long, free reach from the shoulder, with hackney gait the rare exception. Meander Whippets were slightly larger than most Whippets found in America during the 1930s. As a group they had better bone, balance and a more elegant outline giving the appearance of a true sporting Hound. Ch. Mica, Ch. Michael, Ch. Slag of Meander and Ch. Red Wagon were among the largest of the early Meander Whippets. Mica, Slag and Red Wagon weighed 28 to 29 pounds at full maturity with Michael being a bit larger at about 30 pounds.

The development of Meander-type or American-type Whippets was strictly a breeding program operated by careful selection of brood stock by Julia and Judy Shearer. Ch. Sandbrilliant was an English import. Much of the early brood stock purchased was heavy in English blood. It was the ability of the Shearer sisters to select outstanding individuals for their breeding program, not whether a Whippet was American- or English-bred. The Shearer's culled heavily, making few comments to the outside

35

The dogs shown here were the foundation of the American-type Whippet. Ch. Sandbrilliant of Meander (extreme left) and Ch. Syndicate of Meander (extreme right) were the sire and dam of the eight champions between them. They are (from left) Mica, Carbon Copy, Woodland Princess, Thelma, Slag, Feet, Syndic and Slate, all of Meander. *George.*

Whippet world when failures occurred. Few Whippet breeders in America had the courage or money to follow such a pattern of keeping only the best.

Ch. Sandbrilliant of Meander was not a large Whippet. The first time I saw him exhibited was at the Maryland Kennel Club Show in Baltimore, where he went BB. He was the most beautiful, well-balanced Whippet I had ever seen and left with me my first memory of what constituted the ideal. As time went on and Whippets became slightly larger, both the Shearers and I believed that Ch. Sandbrilliant was a bit on the small, delicate-appearing side as compared to some of his offspring. A revision of the Whippet Standard on June 2, 1934 on height, stating "Dogs 18 to 20 inches—Bitches 17 to 18 inches," was a clear indication the Whippet in America was growing larger, as compared to his English counterparts.

Ch. Mica of Meander was by far the best showman ever exhibited by Miss Julia Shearer. He performed on many occasions without the use of a lead in the show ring. Mica would pose untouched with an alert expression which was virtually unheard of at the time. Like many Meander Whippets, Mica had beautifully constructed, well-knuckled cat feet with a slight bend of the strong pasterns going into the foot. These were not the little cat feet often seen today in Whippets with long straight pasterns similar to the Fox Terrier, and not suitable to give proper grip for racing on a track. Ch. Mica of Meander was perhaps the best specimen ever produced by Meander Kennels as having the ideal conformation and temperament for both show ring and race track. Mica put it all together in filling the eye.

Post-Depression Racing

Whippet racing around Baltimore continued to grow as America slowly recovered from the effects of the Depression. Many of the Whippets quartered at the track kennel at Brooklandville were growing too old for racing. People living in the Baltimore—Washington area started purchasing Whippets for racing at Brooklandville. This quickly changed the pattern from an operation where the track controlled most of the racing Whippets to an operation where individual owners who did not kennel at the track supplied most of the racers. There were no regular purses, but there was betting available through bookmakers who operated at the track. Betting was orderly and smart owners could make money. Whippets in the Depression years of the 1930s had greater dollar value and demand around Baltimore than the race Whippet of the 1970s under ever-increasing inflation. The reason was simply that betting gave the owner an opportunity to expect some small profit from his racer.

William Kelly, the first kennelmaster at the Maryland Whippet Club Track at Brooklandville left the track to establish a boarding and grooming business. In 1932, Bill Kelly, assisted by another Whippet owner, Mr. W. C. Summner and his son, opened a second track known as Southern Maryland Whippet Club, Chesapeake Beach, Calvert County, Maryland. The Depression was at full strength, yet there were two Whippet tracks operating in opposition to each other. Both showed a reasonable profit for the season. All Whippet racing was now held at night under flood lights.

An important change that benefitted Whippet racing most in this period was the dropping of the system of handicapping Whippets by weight. The absurd weight handicap system was abolished and dogs were given yard advantages based on speed, ability and/or time. The track handicapper determined the yard advantage of each Whippet. The fastest Whippet would start at scratch marked (X), or would run a full 200 yards. The Whippet having the second fastest time or was considered "second best," would get yards advantage over the scratch Whippet marked (X). A race handicapped on ability or time and based on yards, might be like this: *Post Position #1* Marked "X"—200 yards, *Post Position #2*-3 yards advantage—197 yards, *Post Position #3-* 6 yards advantage—194 yards, *Post Position #4*-7 yards advantage—193 yards, etc. The system of yards advantage, based on speed, required keen knowledge by the track handicapper and bettors. Bookmakers could go broke if there was not a thorough understanding of the yard handicap system and the betting odds offered to the public on each dog.

Electric starting boxes now replaced hand slipping at the start of a race. Each starting box was placed in a race lane based on the yard handicap received by the racer. A Whippet given a 3-yard advantage would have the starting box placed at the 197 yard mark, etc. Owners still ran down the track from the starting box to the finish line and attracted the attention of their dogs at the finish line by calling and waving a cloth. The drag-type of lure had not yet come into operation.

Those owners playing a major part in Whippet racing were Felix Lesser, Phyllis Poe, Betty Glen, Homer Ambrose, Louis Pegram, Philip L. Poe, John A. Hatfield, Charles Brawner, Herman Duker, M. Nelson Bond, W. Kyser Manley, Dr. John Engel, Margaret Little, George Brian, Jr., William Kelly, W. C. Summner, Dudley Brown, L. Fink, Jim Rowe, R. Yarrington and W. H. Jones.

Average weight of all Whippets racing at Brooklandville and Chesapeake Beach averaged 18.93 pounds per racer. Show standards in England and America talked in terms of height at the shoulder, weight was the common standard of size used by both the show and race groups in Maryland.

Outstanding racers during this period were: Fire Bell, Summner's Beauty, Slim Chance, Veda, Gallant Fox, Summner's Gypsy, Fire Chief,

William Kelly with two racers of the 1930s, Blue Bell (left) and Blue Boy.

A field of racers at the finish line, Brooklandville, 1930.

Ch. Galloping Ghost, Sonny Boy, My Own, Fag O Bella, Errand Boy, Black Fox, Bounding Deep, Sir Hector, Bar Maid, Blue Maid, Try Me, Brooklyn Boy, Try Connal Go Bragh, Merry Legs, Rogue, and Ravenell.

The big break for Whippet racing in Maryland came in 1935 when the Arundel Kennel Club, Riviera Beach, Maryland operated the first circular Whippet track. Greyhound racing was being held at the Auditorium in Atlantic City, New Jersey but was suddenly closed down by the State of New Jersey without warning. The group that built the Atlantic City track came to Maryland and built a circular track identical in size to the Atlantic City oval. Whippets took to the circular track racing with little or no training after racing on the straight track. Distance proved no problem for Whippets with nightly races over distances of ⅛ mile, 280 yards, 440 yards, and 550 yards. There was local option betting and crowds flocked to the track. All went too well for the first circular Whippet track, and after less than two summers of operations, this track was closed. It left an unforgettable memory with Whippet owners as we had felt the profit and thrills of seeing Whippets perform at high speeds over a distance of ground on a circular track. Races were held three to five nights a week with eight to ten races nightly and six Whippets to a race.

Those Whippets who proved outstanding in circular racing were Ch. Red Wagon, Tippity Witchett, Flying Heels, Gallant Lady, Golden Time, Golden Fly, Merry Time, Omaha, Queen, Happy Helen, King Saxon, Mickey Mouse, and Chase Me.

Leading owners were W. C. Summner, William J. Kelly, Clinton and Dale Cole, Jim Flynn, Louis Pegram, Al and Joe Cesky, Carl Eiffert, Dr. John Engel, George Radcliffe, Edward Reimer, George Spangler, G. W. Paggett, Jack Wilson, Red and Towny Capp, Teddy Cox, and Mrs. Theodore Pedersen.

Meander Kennels did not race and often objected to Whippet racing. The Meander-bred Whippets were outstanding in circular track racing, chasing the electric lure. Meander Whippets never favored rag racing, and were vastly superior when chasing the life-like rabbit lure around the circular track. Over 20 Meander-bred Whippets raced with success at this meeting.

Local Option Betting

There was great enthusiasm for Whippet racing after the summer season had closed at the Arundel Kennel Club Track. The Sports Center on the corner of North Avenue and Charles Street, Baltimore, Maryland, was available for rent. We attempted local option betting and a circular track was built in the area where ice skating had been held. Little was known about making electric circular track lures, so on opening night, we had lure problems along with the legal test on local option betting.

At 8:30 p.m. it was time for the first race. Red Wagon was in the first race. The lure was started well ahead of the dogs but was not fast enough and Red Wagon won the race some 10 lengths ahead of the lure and the rest of the field. The police then stepped in at the finish and said, "No more racing." None of us went to jail, but this did end our attempt for local option betting in Baltimore. Such tests as these required dedication to the sport of Whippet racing. All of us who had raced a Whippet prior to the stopping of the races by the police, were subject to jail and fines. We had both lawyers and bondsmen present, but they were not needed.

All Whippet owners, track operators, and employees knew they were subject to arrest or fines during the 1920s, 1930s and 1940s, where bookmaking and local option betting was allowed. We accepted this, and conducted the sport properly. There has never been an arrest for racing Whippets connected with gambling, but there were periods when political pressure made it "too hot" to race.

Many Whippet owners today might not understand why betting made better Whippet racing, and greater objectivity between Whippet owners. The bookmaker or track operating under local option betting always allowed in setting betting odds on a race a certain amount of profit to operate the track, and a profit for themselves. This type of betting is known as operating a "balanced book," or a profit on every race above the amount bet. The same policy is followed today by horse and Greyhound tracks where mutuel betting is allowed. Track take is from 12c to 17c from each dollar bet, depending on the terms of the law governing racing in a State where legal racing is held. Generally about half of the above amount goes to the State, and the other half to the track owners to cover cost of maintaining track, purse money, profit and other expenses.

All major newspapers in Baltimore and the Washington, D.C. area carried daily Whippet race entries and results. Feature stories and pictures of race Whippets were the general rule. You were proud to own a race Whippet in the 1930s and 1940s.

Racing Refinements

Maryland Whippet Club, at Brooklandville, was the only track operating in the State after the closing of the Arundel Kennel Club in 1936. The Brooklandville Track still offered 200-yard races on a straight course with lanes for each starter. There was no mechanical lure and Whippets were attracted in each race by the owner running down the track waving a cloth and calling the dog at the finish line. This form of racing was now obsolete after circular track racing with an electric lure propelling a stuffed rabbit on an arm, plus a modern Greyhound-type starting box were introduced.

The kennel building at the Brooklandville track where racing dogs were boarded. This was the first facility of its kind and was in use in 1933.

Sweet Afton, considered the fastest rough-coated Whippet ever to race in Maryland.

A typical race Whippet of the early 1930s. This dog weighed 21½ pounds.

Management of the Brooklandville Track quickly realized that Whippet owners and spectators would no longer accept rag racing. Charles Brawner and Raleigh Burrows built a straight track drag lure with the use of an axle and motor from an old automobile that would drag the lure down the center of the 200-yard track just ahead of the racers. This was an improvement over calling Whippets at the finish line and waving a cloth. Lanes were discarded and starting boxes were grouped together. The system of giving yard advantage, based on time and/or ability was discarded. There were enough Whippets available for races based on equal racing ability, so that six Whippets of approximately equal speed could start from one starting box. The grading system used was very similar to the one now in use by the American Whippet Club on a national basis and by all Greyhound tracks in America.

Once people had seen circular track Whippet racing, on a large track, interest continued to drop off in straightaway racing with a mechanical lure. By 1939, the Maryland Whippet Club converted to the circular track with races at 165 yards, 265 yards, and 385 yards. A second track was built in Arundel County in 1941 known as the Stoney Creek Whippet Club. Both tracks offered eight to 10 races nightly with six Whippets to a race. Both tracks also offered betting, one through bookmakers, and the other with mutuel windows. Management of both tracks controlled the betting. The effects of the Depression had become largely an unpleasant memory, and business was again starting to boom as a result of World War II.

Outstanding racers on these two circular tracks were Canadian Prince, Merry Fly, Coon Country, Happy Wagon, Orient Express, Miss Magellan, Rackem Up, Minney Mouse II, Cloudy Weather, Gangster of Meander, Heelfly, Golden Time, Black Trouble, Finis La Guerre II, Omaha, Mystery Maid, Calumet Dick, Mexborough, Traveler, Queen of Spades, Major Blacktail, Sea Biscuit, and Sir Echo.

The most active owners at this time were Vic Sprecher, Betty Lee Hinks, Clinton A. Coale, George Radcliffe, Frank Murray, Calvin Weiss, William Bergtold, William Ward, Edward Cooper, Charles Brawner, Louis Pegram, Bob and Mary Quante, Louis (Buddy) Rosenhein, Mrs. Theodore Pedersen, Jack Wilson, Dr. A. Schwarzkopf, Jack Cory, Jack Schley, Gilbert Tracey, Nick Troyer, William Kelly, Dr. J. E. Knoblock, Barbara Lee Goldberg, Forrest Crutcher, R. O. Godar, Dr. John Moss, Al Feast, Dale Cole, Mrs. Eleanor Kapp, Al and Joe Cesky, Merle Feltenberger, Raleigh Burrows, George Grogan, Gilbert Troyer, Marvin and Dolly Goldberg, Sherman Ensor, George Cummings, Frank T. Kapp, Jr., William Muth and Homer Ambrose.

Official Program

The Brooklandville Kennel Club

BROOKLANDVILLE, MD.

TUES. OCTOBER 5, 1943

Price 15 Cents

First Race—9:00 P. M.

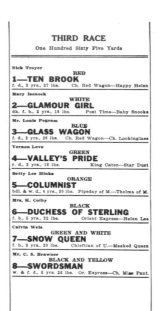

THIRD RACE
One Hundred Sixty Five Yards

Nick Troyer
RED
1—TEN BROOK
f. d., 3 yrs., 27 lbs.   Ch. Red Wagon—Happy Helen

Mary Isenock
WHITE
2—GLAMOUR GIRL
dk. f. b., 2 yrs., 18 lbs.   Post Time—Baby Snooks

Mr. Louis Pegram
BLUE
3—GLASS WAGON
f. d., 2 yrs., 26 lbs.   Ch. Red Wagon—Ch. Lookinglass

Vernon Love
GREEN
4—VALLEY'S PRIDE
r. d., 2 yrs., 18 lbs.   King Caton—Star Dust

Betty Lee Hinks
ORANGE
5—COLUMNIST
bdl. & w. d., 4 yrs., 20 lbs.   Pipeday of M.—Thelma of M.

Mrs. K. Colby
BLACK
6—DUCHESS OF STERLING
f. b., 5 yrs., 22 lbs.   Orient Express—Helen Lee

Calvin Weis
GREEN AND WHITE
7—SNOW QUEEN
f. b., 3 yrs., 20 lbs.   Chieftian of U.—Masked Queen

Mr. C. S. Brawner
BLACK AND YELLOW
8—SWORDSMAN
w. & f. d., 6 yrs. 26 lbs.   Or. Express—Ch. Miss Pant.

Official Program
—
Maryland Whippet Club

BROOKLANDVILLE, MD.

Friday, October 14, 1932

Price 10 Cents

THIRD RACE

ALLOWANCES:
Two Hundred Yards

Danskill Kennels
RED
1—BROOKLYN BOY   X
b. d., 4, 19 lbs.   Midnight—Glenochie

Walter B. Brooks, Jr.
WHITE
2—CALGARY SILVER   4 Yds.
f. d., 3, 16 lbs.   Ch. Taffy's Pride—Ch. Victory Flying Mistress

Miss Betty Glenn
BLUE
3—BETTY G   5 Yds.
b., 2, 21 lbs.   Rye & Soda—Gin Rickey

Roland Kennels
GREEN
4—BAR MAID   7 Yds.
b. b., 2, 17 lbs.   Rye & Soda—Gin Rickey

Chestnut Hill Kennels
YELLOW
5—MAINSHEET   11 Yds.
b. d., 3, 14 lbs.   Cal. Carroll—Blue Bell

Mt. Vernon Kennels
BLACK
6—WHITEFOOT   20 Yds.
b. d., 6, 16 lbs.   Golong Galloping—Tinker Bell

Remember that a finish viewed from an angle is usually very deceptive, and that the Judges—who were selected for their skill and integrity—are in the best position to determine the result of a close race.

Official programs for races of the Brooklandville Kennel Club and the Maryland Whippet Club. Both Clubs held races on the Brooklandville facility.

OFFICIAL PROGRAM

— —

SOUTHERN MARYLAND WHIPPET CLUB

TRACK:

On the State Road near

CHESAPEAKE BEACH

Calvert County, Maryland

TUESDAY, JUNE 14, 1932

Price 10 Cents

THIRD RACE

Allowances: Purse to Winner and Second
Two Hundred Yards

Dudley Browne
RED
1—FIRE BELL X
$300
f. b., 25 lbs., 2 yrs. Sumner's Tom—Ceta Keck

W. C. Sumner
WHITE
2—SUMNER'S BEAUTY X
$300
blk. b., 14½ lbs., 5 yrs. Dick—Another Try

W. J. Kelly
BLUE
3—SLIM CHANCE 3 YDS.
$100
brd. d., 18 lbs., 3 yrs.

W. C. Sumner
GREEN
4—KOON KAHN 6 YDS.
$200
blk. d., 20 lbs., 3 yrs. Sum's Tom—Merit

Mr. L. Fink
YELLOW
5—PIQUANT PORKER 7 Yds.
$150
f. d., 18½ lbs., 5 yrs. Ch. Gal. Ghost—Blue Maid

Mrs. Spangler
BLACK
6—MISHAP 8 YDS.
$200
r. b., 20 lbs., 4 yrs. Sum's Blazer—Flash

Remember that a finish viewed from an angle
is usually very deceptive, and that the Judges—
who were selected for their skill and integrity—
are in the best position to determine the result
of a close race.

Official program of a claiming race held by the Southern Maryland Whippet club. Claiming prices are included with the vital statistics of each entry.

OFFICIAL PROGRAM

AND

PAST PERFORMANCES

ARUNDEL KENNEL CLUB

RIVIERA BEACH

July 3, 1935

PRICE 15 CENTS

EIGHTH RACE
280 Yards

		Track	Date	Dist.	Time	P.P.	Str.	Fin.	Order of Finish
1 1701 RED	**FLYING HEELS**								Owner—Satyr Hill Heels
	F. D., 3 yrs., 26 lbs., Piper—Lightning Flash								
		RB.	6-29-35	F.C.	26.1	7	2	2²	Tip. Wit. 2, Fl. Heels 10, Rogue 12
		RB.	6-27-35	F.C.	27.1	3	4	3	Tip. Wit. 1, D. Girl 2, Fl. Heels 1
		RB.	6-26-35	F.C.		4	5	3	Red Wagon ½, Tip. Wit. 10, Fl. Heels 1
		RB.	9-15-34	F.C.	26.1	8	3	3⁴	Dream G. 3, Tip. Wit. 1, Fly. Heels 3
2 1702 WHITE	**DREAM GIRL**								Owner—Park Heights Kennels
	B. B., 2 yrs., 24 lbs., Bounding Deep—Merry Legs								
		RB.	6-27-35	F.C.	27.1	5	2	1	Tip. Wit. 1, D. Girl 2, Fl. Heels 1
		RB.	9-15-34	F.C.	26.1	6	6	1¹	D. Girl 3, Tip. Wit. 2, Fly Heel
3 1703 BLUE	**BAR MAID**								Owner—Holland Kennels
	F. B., 5 yrs., 23 lbs., Rye & Soda—Gin Rickey								
		RB.	6-20-35	F.C.	26.1	6	3	4²⁰	Tip. Wit. 2, Fl. Heels 10, Rogue 12
		RB.	6-27-35	F.C.	27.1	2	2	4	Tip. Wit. 1, D. Girl 2, Fl. Heels 1
		RB.	6-26-35	F.C.	27.2	1	2	2	Rogue ns, Bar M. 6, W. Jack hd
		RB.	6-23-35	½	15.1	1	1	1½	B. Maid ½, Chase Me 2, W. Count
4 1704 YELLOW	**TIPPITY WITCHETT**								Owner—Sea Girt Kennels
	Br. D., 2 yrs., 21 lbs., Merry Legs—Bounding Deep								
		RB.	6-29-35	F.C.	26.1	3	1	1²	Tip. Wit. 2, Fl. Heels 10, Rogue 12
		RB.	6-27-35	F.C.	27.1	4	3	1	Tip. Wit. 1, D. Girl 2, Fl. Heels 1
		RB.	6-26-35	F.C.	26.1	6	1	2¹⁰	R. Wagon ½, Tip. Wit. 10, Fl. Heels 1
		RB.	9-15-34	F.C.	26.1	1	2	2³	D. Girl 3, Tip. Wit. 1, Fl. Heels 3
5 1705 GREEN	**RED WAGON**								Owner—Louis Pegram, Jr.
	F. & W. D., 2 yrs., 29 lbs., Scepter of Meander—Thelma of Meander								
		RB.	6-28-35	F.C.	25.1	7	1	1⁴	R. Wagon 12, Tip. Wit. hd, Fl. Heels 5
		RB.	6-26-35	F.C.	26.1	2	2	1	Red Wagon ½, Tip. Wit. 10, Fl. Heels 1
		RB.	9-15-34	F.C.	25.2	7	5	1¹	R. Wagon 1, Chase Me 5, Merit
6 1706 BLACK	**GALLANT LADY**								Owner—Satyr Hills Kennels
	Br. & W. B., 2 yrs., 14½ lbs., Faga B.—Fl. Mamie								
		RB.	6-29-35	F.C.	26.1	2	5	5²¹	Tip. Wit. 2, Fl. Heels 10, Rogue 12
		RB.	6-27-35	F.C.	27.1	3	1	1	G. Lady 2, Chase Me 6, Bradshaw 1
		RB.	6-26-35	F.C.	26.1	8	4	4³	Tip. Wit. 10, Fl. Heels 1
		RB.	6-22-35	½	15.	2	1	1⁵	G. Lady 15, Omaha 6, Ted Clark
7 1707 BUFF	**HIJACKER**								Owner—Geo. Radcliffe
		RB.	6-29-35	280	18.3	7	3	1¹	Hijacker 3, J. Smoke 5, M. Julep 6
		RB.	6-26-35	F.C.	26.1	5	8	5	Red Wagon ½, Tip. Wit. 10, Fl. Heels 1
		RB.	6-26-35	F.C.	26.1	5	8	5⁶	Red Wagon ½, Tip. Wit. 10, Fl. Heels 1
8 1708 PINK	**CHASE ME**								Owner—Oakmont Kennels
	Brd. D., 2 yrs., 24 lbs., Acey Deucey—Cora Marie								
		RB.	6-29-35	F.C.	27.4	8	3	1²	Chase Me 1, Faga Bala hd, Queen 1
		RB.	6-27-35	F.C.	27.1	2	2	2	G. Lady 2, Chase Me 6, Bradshaw 1
		RB.	6-26-35	F.C.	26.1	7	6	8	Red Wagon ½, Tip. Wit. 10, Fl. Heels 1
		RB.	6-23-35	F.C.	27.3	1	1	1	Chase Me, Barmaid (dead heat)

Official program for a race meeting of the Arundel Kennel Club.

The Decline of Racing

World War II had become a reality. Stoney Creek Whippet Club closed, never to open again. Maryland Whippet Club continued on through and past the war years with off and on Whippet racing. By 1947 any hope of reviving Whippet racing with betting and purse money for each race had died. A few owners struggled to keep the sport going on a non-profit basis, but times, laws, and people had changed. By 1950, Baltimore, Maryland, once the Mecca of all Whippet racing in America, was virtually without a Whippet population. The Whippets and their owners seemed to vanish almost overnight leaving only Mrs. Theodore Pedersen, Garden City Kennels, Towson, Maryland, who was to go on from racing to establish a great record in the show ring with her Whippets, most of them with a heavy racing background.

The complete disappearance of Whippets around Baltimore was a great blow to the breed. There were many excellent racing specimens that were vastly superior in conformation to many Whippets in other sections of America where racing had not existed. Temperament was super as these little dogs were handled by lead-out boys going to the starting box, and were completely at home under floodlights in front of the racing public. Many Whippets of today could certainly use their outgoing temperament, plus their great desire to run and win, reflecting the earlier introduction of Terrier blood in establishing the Whippet as a breed. Virtually all racers were house pets. A great number of the early race Whippets were pets, and in many cases sound enough for the show ring.

Those who did not own Whippets in Maryland during the period of 1930 to 1947 missed the truly romantic period of the breed in America. Money was scarce or nonexistent, but hope, objectivity and interest in the Whippet knew no bounds. People owning Whippets at that time were a true cross section and typical of all Americans. Whippet racing had no class boundaries. Any owner who had outstanding Whippets and acted courteously was well-received by the Whippet "industry." You were judged by the quality of your Whippets and your own behavior.

Betting was a necessary part of the game in Whippet racing. During this period, it was necessary for the author to work with every bookmaker and money man who operated at the Maryland Whippet tracks. Bookmakers and track operators were businessmen. At times Whippet owners did not like the betting odds offered on their racers. Realistically, though, if one did not like the odds on his dogs, then the simple thing to do was not to bet.

Welshing on a bet, to the best of my knowledge, never occured after 1935, when Whippet owners and track operators operated as a team. There were a few cases where Whippet owners tried to win bets and in some way attempted to slow-down or speed-up their racers. There were

46

FIFTH RACE

400 yards - - Track Record—Queen of Spades, 27.1

Track	Date	Dist.	Time	P.P.	S.	Str.	Fin.	Order of Finish
1 RED — TEN CROWN								Owner—V. T. Sprucher
R., 3 yrs., Will o' the Wisp—Banwark Lassie								
S.C.	9-17-41	275	20.1	4	4	5	4⁶	Deep Step, Dream Princess, Happy Queen.
S.C.	9-13-41	170	12.	6	1	1	1⁸	Ten Crown, Dream Princess, Dane Lady.
S.C.	9-6-41	275	20.	1	1	3	3⁵	Jerry B., Deep Step, Ten Crown.
S.C.	9-5-41	275	19.2	2	2	2	2¹⁰	Silver Arrow, Ten Crown, Happy Queen.
2 WHITE — ORIENT EXPRESS								Owner—C. Brawner
F., 5 yrs., Ch. Sandbrilliant of Meander—Queen Dido								
S.C.	9-17-41	275	20.1	5	7	7	7⁹	Deep Step, All Pal, Run Read.
S.C.	9-13-41	400	29.1	5	6	6	6²⁰	Gangster, Thaddeus B., Candy Duke.
S.C.	9-12-41	400	28.3	4	6	6	5¹⁷	Merry Fly, Happy Helen, Swordsman.
S.C.	9-10-41	400	28.3	8	6	4	2²	Thaddeus B., Orient Express, Happy Helen.
3 BLUE — HAPPY HELEN								Owner—C. A. Coale
L., F., 7 yrs., Brown Jack—High Brow								
S.C.	9-17-41	400	29.	2	6	5	5⁷	Daily Double, Sir Echo, Masked Queen.
S.C.	9-12-41	400	28.3	2	2	2	2²	Merry Fly, Happy Helen, Swordsman.
S.C.	9-10-41	400	28.3	4	5	2	3³	Thaddeus B., Orient Express, Happy Helen.
S.C.	9-6-41	275	19.1	4	7	5	4⁸	Traveler, Sleepy Time, Pale Hands.
4 GREEN — DOLLY'S PRIDE								Owner—Peterson
BE. & W., 3 yrs., Isadore—Black Monday								
S.C.	9-17-41	275	19.	2	7	5	5¹³	Cloudy Weath., Traveler, Dr. Goodhand.
S.C.	9-13-41	275	19.	5	4	4	4¹⁸	Dapper Dan, Finnis La Guerre, Traveler.
S.C.	9-12-41	400	28.3	3	5	4	4¹⁵	Merry Fly, Happy Helen, Swordsman.
S.C.	9-10-41	400	27.2	5	6	7	7²⁰	Cloudy Weath., Mask, Queen, Daily Double.
5 YELLOW — THADDEUS B.								Owner—Pilgrim Kennels
F., Ch. Slag of Meander—Lightning								
S.C.	9-17-41	275	19.	8	7	6	6¹⁸	Major Blacktail, Time Fly, Merry Fly.
S.C.	9-13-41	400	29.1	6	4	2	2⁴	Gangster, Thaddeus B., Candy Duke.
S.C.	9-10-41	400	28.3	1	7	3	1²	Thaddeus B., Orient Express, Happy Helen.
S.C.	9-3-41	400	29.	4	7	5	5¹⁰	Happy Helen, Orient Express, Lone Rang.
6 BLACK — GANGSTER OF MEANDER								Owner—L. Pagram
F., 2 yrs.								
S.C.	9-17-41	275	19.	5	6	4	4¹²	Major Blacktail, Time Fly, Merry Fly.
S.C.	9-13-41	400	29.1	1	1	1	1¹	Gangster, Thaddeus B., Candy Duke.
S.C.	9-12-41	170	11.3	4	8	5	5¹⁰	Maj. Blacktail, Dr. Goodhand, La Chapelle.
S.C.	9-5-41	275	19.3	4	5	5	5²¹	Silver Arrow, Ten Crown, Happy Queen.
7 ORANGE — STEEL KING								Owner—Hilton Kennels
BE., 2 yrs., War Admiral—Little Lou								
S.C.	9-17-41	275	20.1	8	4	3	4⁸	Deep Step, All Pal, Run Read.
S.C.	9-13-41	275	21.	6	5	6	6¹⁸	Blue Donna, Sir Echo, Candy Pig.
S.C.	9-12-41	400	28.3	6	6	6	6¹³	Queen o' Spades, Daily Double, Carmichael.
S.C.	9-10-41	400	28.3	6	4	5	5⁷	Thaddeus B., Orient Express, Happy Helen.
8 PURPLE — CANDY DUKE								Owner—F. Vlack
W. BD., 2 yrs., Coco Country—Candy Pig								
S.C.	9-17-41	170	12.	6	6	6	6¹¹	Bound, Judge, Maj. Minor, Lone Ranger.
S.C.	9-13-41	400	29.1	2	3	3	3¹²	Gangster, Thaddeus B., Candy Duke.
S.C.	9-12-41	400	28.	3	6	5	5¹³	Queen o' Spades, Daily Double, Carmichael.
S.C.	9-10-41	170	12.1	2	8	8	7¹⁰	Carmichael, Lone Ranger, Dr. Goodhand.

Official program—Stoney Creek Whippet Club.

SEVENTH RACE

Two Hundred Sixty Yards — Record, 15.3—King Saxon

	Date / Race Dist. Time PP Off Str Fin.				Starts	1	2	3	Order of Finish
1 RED — Audrey Joan Burroughs — MEXBOROUGH	f d, w 2-35, 26 lbs.				6	0	1	1	Tipgely Witchett / Kerry Patch
6-27-N	450	27.2	6	4	4-15				Orient Express, Candy Queen
6-23-7	260	19.	3	2	2-4				Calgary Tim, Maj. Blacktail
6-20-7	150	10.3	4	1	3-4				Fly. Heels II, Calgary Tim
6-16-N	270	27.	4	4	4-10				Traveler, Happy Helen
6-7	260	19.2	8	2	.. 6				Traveler, Omaha
2 WHITE — Charles S. Brawner — ORIENT EXPRESS	f d, w 8-26, 25 lbs.				7	2	1	0	Ch. Sandbrilliant of Meander / Queen Dido
6-27-N	450	27.2	1	1	1-8				Candy Queen, Maj. Blacktail
6-23-7	260	19.	1	1	4-5				Calgary Tim, Mexborough
6-20-7	260	19.	1	1	5-6				Fly. Heel, Calgary Tim
6-16-N	260	19.3	5	7	5-6				Headshaw, Flying Heels II
6-9-7	260	19.2	8	7	5-10				Happy Helen, Flying Heels II
3 BLUE — H. A. Nicholson — TRAVELER	f d, w 8-35, 28 lbs.				7	2	0	1	Piper / Kerry Patch
6-23-N	260	19.2	5	3	1-3				Flying Heels, Happy Helen
6-16-N	270	27.	2	5	1-4				Traveler, Happy Helen, Heelfly
6-9-4	270	27.2	3	3	3-2				Merry Time, Omaha
6-8-N	270	27.	4	3	1				Traveler, Omaha
6-7-N	370	26.2	5	7	3-9				Brown Buddy, Canadian Prince
4 GREEN — Winsome Kennels — ME O MY	r & w b, w 12-35, 30 lbs.				3	0	0	1	King Saxon / June Bride
6-23-N	260	19.2	7	6	6-6				Flying Heels, Happy Helen
6-16-N	370	22.	2	2	7				Traveler, Omaha
5-30-N	370	27.2	4	4	4-8				Orient Express, Silver Nose
5-218	150	10.3	1	1	1-4				Moon Country, Long Tom, Jr.
5 YELLOW — Bel Air Kennels — HEEL FLY	f d, w 11-35, 24 lbs.				4	2	0	1	s.h. Red Wagon / Helen Lee
5-20-N	270	27.	2	1	1-4				Brown Buddy, On Sir
6-16-N	270	27.	3	2	2-7				Traveler, Happy Helen
6-9-4	270	27.2	7	6	5				Merry Time, Omaha
5-26-N	270	26.2	1	1	1-10				Omaha, Brown Buddy
†Formerly Red Heim.									
6 BLACK — Jack Schley — MERRY TIME	r d, 5-23, 35 lbs.				4	1	0	0	Bounding Home / Merry Legs
6-20-N	370	27.3	5	ran out					Heel Fly, Brown Buddy
6-16-N	370	27.	6	2	5-10				Traveler, Happy Helen
6-9-4	370	27.2	4	1	1-2				Omaha, Traveler
5-26-N	370	26.2	7	6	6-21				Heel Fly, Omaha
5-78		10.4	..	2	1-2				Omaha, Major Blacktail
7 ORANGE — Forrest Kennels — Canadian PRINCE	f d, w 3-26, 30 lbs.				5	2	1	0	Shoemaker / Young Kitty
6-23-N	260	19.	8	7	7-4				Flying Heels, Traveler
6-16-N	270	27.	1	1	5				Traveler, Happy Helen
6-9-4	370	27.2	6	4	4				Brown Buddy, Traveler
6-3-N	370	26.2	6	1	3-5				Brown Buddy, Traveler
5-26-7	260	19.4	2	1	1				On Sir, Dream Princess
8 PURPLE — Mrs. Mildred Cosky — OMAHA	w & f d, w 12-24, 37 lbs.				4	0	2	0	Faga Bala / Moon Blondie
6-9-4	370	27.2	1	2	2-2				Merry Time, Traveler
6-8-N	370	27.	3	4	1				Traveler, Omaha
5-26-N	370	26.2	2	1	6-13				Brown Buddy, Canadian Prince
5-26-N	370	26.2	8	4	2-10				Heelfly, Brown Buddy
5-218	370	26.	1	1	1				Alone

Official program—Brooklandville Kennel Club.

also a few cases of "ringers" or substituting one Whippet that looked like another. These instances were few and the great majority of Whippet owners frowned upon such tactics. As time went by the owners of Whippet tracks actually hired certain of the Whippet owners to control identification, judging, etc. The author was one of the first to be paid a nightly salary to help coordinate problems that existed between owners and track management. Nightly attendance at the Maryland Whippet tracks ran from 500 to 4,000 people. It was most important that there be a minimum of confusion.

Whippet Breeders Association of Maryland

The largest and best-organized Whippet Club in America with great influence on all Whippet activities was the Whippet Breeders Association of Maryland, Inc. This Club had great strength and membership truly represented a cross section of American society of the time. Doctors, lawyers, successful businessmen and people in all walks of life belonged. Members of the WBAM developed modern track equipment, a registration bureau for all track Whippets, and a grading system equal in efficiency to that of the Greyhound industry. The WBAM was the power factor in Whippets through the 1940s. The American Whippet Club was national in scope, but operated strictly as a Virginia-New York-supervised organization with major emphasis on one Eastern Specialty show each year.

The American Kennel Club registered only 36 Whippets in 1934, clearly indicating that many Whippets were not being registered. The major survival factor of the Whippet during the Depression years was directly due to Whippet racing and activities of the WBAM. During the period 1930 to 1948, the great majority of all Whippets in America were located in Maryland or owned by Meander Kennels which was less than 120 miles from Baltimore.

The WBAM supported many activities to stimulate interest in Whippets. It was through its efforts that established Whippet tracks started paying purses on each race. It took a strike against the tracks to accomplish this end, but we won. It became apparent that local option betting on Whippets was very risky at best. On two occasions the WBAM sponsored bills in the Maryland Legislature to legalize betting on Whippets. We failed by only one vote in the first attempt. The second attempt was a disaster when Greyhound track money appeared, and a combined effort by horse tracks, tobacco interests and churches thoroughly defeated the Whippet bill. Great credit for the attempts to legalize Whippet racing must go to the entire membership of the organization, especially to Dr. John Engel, Mr. Clinton A. Coale and a young lawyer, Mr. Jerome Robin-

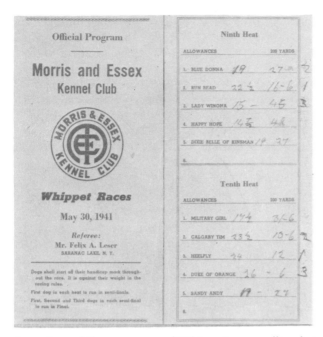

A portion of the program of Whippet races offered at
the Morris and Essex show in 1941.

Ch. Stoney Meadows Masquerade, owned and bred by Mr. and Mrs. W. Potter
Wear, won his first BIS at the Suffolk County Kennel Club under Mrs. William
H. Long, Jr. Mrs. Newcombe was Club President at the time (1950) and is
shown presenting the trophy. *Brown.*

son, who is now a judge in the State of Maryland. The chief attention-getter at the first hearing on the bill for legalization of Whippet racing was the appearance of Ch. Red Wagon before the House of Representatives. Just as is the case today, many members of the legislature said, "What is a Whippet?" The question, of course, was answered by Red Wagon.

The WBAM sponsored an annual combined race meeting and sanction match which drew larger Whippet entries than the American Whippet Club Specialty or major all breed shows. Top quality judges and breeder judges were always invited. Miss Julia Shearer, Miss Judith Shearer, Mr. Louis Pegram, Mrs. Winifred Little (now Mrs. Heckmann), Mr. Harry B. Dillehunt, Mr. Cary W. Lindsay and Miss Betty Lee Hinks have all officiated at these affairs. Numerous exhibition race meetings were held at all-breed shows. The late George Foley, President of the Foley Dog Show Organization, was a strong backer of Whippet racing as a spectator attraction. The WBAM annually supported the entry at the Maryland Kennel Club Show in Baltimore. In 1944, under judge Marion Foster Florsheim, an outstanding breeder of Afghans, the Whippet entry was 86 with no extra classes. It was not until the late 1960s and the 1970s that this record entry was exceeded at several of the American Whippet Club Specialties. Again, on the Silver Anniversary of the Maryland Kennel Club, the largest entry ever for a racing class was judged by Mr. Alva Rosenberg. Silver dollars in silver-spangled bags were the prizes to the class winners.

Racing at Morris and Essex

On May 30, 1941, Mrs. Geraldine Dodge offered Whippet racing at the Morris and Essex Kennel Club Show. This was the largest all-breed show of the period and a great showcase for purebred dogs. Responsible for the groundwork was Mrs. Rosslyn Terhune, dog editor for the *News-Post,* Baltimore, Maryland. The races were on the straightaway, and competition was the WBAM vs. Mr. Frank Tuffley of the Cleveland Whippet Club. Maryland was running two circular tracks at the time with over 200 Whippets trained for circular racing. Cleveland appeared on the scene with the old, small-type Whippet of the late 1920s including some rough-coated individuals. It was a complete rout for Cleveland with the Baltimore group making virtually a clean sweep of the $1,000.00 in purse money offered by Mrs. Dodge. Heelfly, by Ch. Pegram's Red Wagon out of Helen Lee, fastest straightaway Whippet of his time, took down first honors, being undefeated during the entire program. The Morris and Essex Show marked the first time I had ever shown under Miss Betty West, now Mrs. Philip S. P. Fell. It rained all day in torrents; thus, all of us taking part in Whippet activities were thoroughly soaked by the end of the day. It was great fun and a great day to honor the all-around Whippet.

Meredith Pegram with the memorable Ch. Pegram's Red Wagon, the first Whippet that enjoyed equal success on the race track, in the show ring and as a pet.

The author's show and racing string of the mid-1930s. Shown are (from bottom) Ch. Pegram's Red Wagon, Yeah Man and Red Patch.

Members of the Cleveland Whippet Club held the final American Whippet Derby on September 28, 1941. The WBAM was invited to attend, but only a small portion of the membership made the long trip to the Hunting Valley Polo Field, Cleveland, Ohio. This time the races were more even, but many of the better track dogs remained in Maryland.

The Establishment of Mardomere

The entry into the Whippet fancy of Mardomere Kennels owned by Mrs. George Anderson, Glen Head, New York, in the early 1940s greatly strengthened show ring competition. Mrs. Anderson called me long distance, stating she was a breeder and exhibitor of Cocker Spaniels and wanted to purchase a Whippet. Not having the slightest idea with whom I was talking, my first question was, "Mrs. Anderson, is $50.00 too much?" She replied, "No, but I want a Whippet for the show ring that can win." Ups and Downs Kennels, owned by Mr. and Mrs. John Doeller had just burned to the ground, and most of these Whippets were available for sale. Mrs. Winnie Little (now Mrs. Heckmann) handled for the Doellers at the time and was keeping some of the dogs temporarily. I told Mrs. Anderson about a young, all-white bitch that should finish easily. She drove down to Baltimore the next weekend and purchased the bitch. Mr. Percy Roberts handled for Mrs. Anderson, and a few months later the newly purchased Snow White of Ups and Downs was shown under me at Annapolis, and was Best of Winners for her first major. Ch. Mica of Meander was my choice for Best of Breed.

Mardomere Kennels quickly dominated the Whippet ring at many Eastern shows, especially in New York, Connecticut, Massachusetts and New Jersey. Percy Roberts, then a handler, purchased a number of imports for Mardomere with the litter sisters, Madam Superb and Lady Bibi, becoming immediate successes. Soon after this Mardomere obtained the outstanding show bitch, Ch. Flornell Glamorous. This bitch was one of the most perfectly balanced Whippets the author had ever seen and quickly made an outstanding record at many major all-breed shows. Selection and handling of early Mardomere Whippets was by Percy Roberts, with advice from a few personal friends of Mrs. Anderson. Harry Murphy and Jack Simm later supervised the kennel and handled for Mardomere in the show ring.

There was great rivalry between Mardomere Kennels and Meander Kennels for top show honors in America. Meander Kennels showed "American type" dogs while Mardomere favored the type more acceptable to the average English Whippet fancier. Meander Whippets were slightly larger than Mardomere Whippets. In most cases it was American type vs. English type. Many times these kennels would sidestep each oth-

Margaret Anderson, whose Mardomere Kennels exerted a powerful influence on the breed for many years, with four of her early winners. They are (from left) Ch. Flornell Glamorous, Fawn Dandy, Ch. Lady Bibi and Ch. Madam Superb.

Brown.

Ch. Lady Bibi was the first Whippet to become an American BIS winner. She is shown taking the top award at the Lenox Kennel Club in 1939 under James Spring, Percy Roberts handling. *Jones.*

er, especially under judges who had strong opinions on type. Meander Whippets were handled in the ring by their owners while Mardomere generally used professional handlers. It was often difficult for small exhibitors to compete against the large show strings of both kennels from 1940 to 1955. When Mardomere or Meander did not show, there were few championship points available. When they did show, they usually took the points and Best of Breed. Many exhibitors during this period carried extra dogs for extra points. The Whippet was still a small breed in number, and often the cheapest way to finish a champion would be to carry your own points with you.

Mardomere Kennels did much to improve overall quality of the Whippet in the show ring, but was virtually a closed kennel operation. Stud services or making brood stock and puppies available to outsiders who might wish to improve their own stock with addition of Mardomere blood lines was a rare occurrence. In a few cases Mardomere did exchange or sell brood stock to a very few selected individuals and in almost every case, Mardomere blood lines carried on well.

Mardomere Kennels was perhaps the most beautiful and largest Whippet kennel in America. The average kennel population ran from 50 to 100 dogs. Mrs. Anderson passed away in the late 1960s, but the kennel was carried on by Mr. Anderson for several years following her death. Most of the Whippets were later humanely put to sleep with the exception of a few of the older dogs who were given to close friends as pets.

The Non-Physical Period

The period following World War II to 1955 could be considered the non-physical period of Whippet development in America. There was no Whippet racing, but fanciers did not object to the Whippet being complete, based on show, race and pet qualities. The popular rivalries between Whippet fanciers of the period were: 1) very small Whippets (English Standard) vs. larger Whippets (American Standard); 2) show Whippets vs. race Whippets; 3) individual prestige of some established fanciers vs. entrance of new Whippet enthusiasts and 4) social and wealth factors creating unnecessary "snobbism." All of these factors added up to great obstacles in trying to establish the Whippet on a sound basis as an all-around dog. Even today it is difficult to overcome these unnecessary, non-objective, personal opinions that greatly hinder increasing growth of the Whippet on a sound basis as an ideal pet, show and race dog.

The non-physical period of growth of the Whippet in America found Meander Kennels and Mardomere Kennels still the major factors in show ring activity. Mrs. Theodore Pedersen, of Garden City Kennels, came to America from Belgium bringing Whippets from that country with her.

Ch. White Iris of Mardomere. *Tauskey*

Ch. Lucky Penny of Mardomere. *Brown*

Ch. Solitaire of Mardomere. *Brown*

These Whippets, all owned by Mardomere Kennels, were noted BIS winners.

Ch. Garden City Sleepy Mouse, owned, bred and handled by Mrs. Theodore Pedersen, was a top winner in the early 1950s. He is shown scoring BIS at the Rock Creek Kennel Club, 1951 under Winifred L. Heckmann.

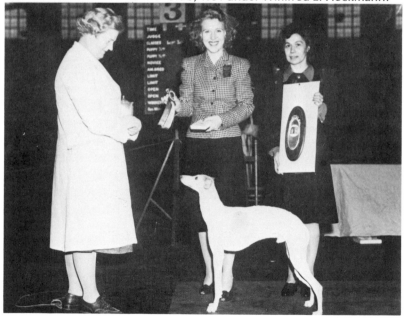

The Whippet entry at the Maryland KC show, 1944 was supported by the WBAM. The entry of 86 was the largest in America to its time. Ch. Ptarmigan of Meander, owned and bred by Meander Kennels was BB under Marion F. Florsheim, Judith Shearer handling.

These Whippets met with success in racing but did not show to the same advantage in the breed ring. When racing came to an end in Maryland, Mrs. Pedersen devoted all of her efforts to conformation. Her success from a rather small group of Whippets was immediate with the most outstanding winner being Ch. Garden City Sleepy Mouse, 78 times shown, 10 BIS, 62 BB, 41 GR1s and 15 GR2s. Mr. Colin Studds' Birdneck Point Kennels, Virginia Beach, Virginia, were prominent in the Eastern show ring for a brief period. Birdneck Point Whippets crossed well with other families of the period with Baron of Birdneck Point being the best producing male from the kennel.

The two most successful kennels developed during the period were Stoney Meadows Kennels, Cecilton, Maryland, owned by Mr. and Mrs. W. Potter Wear and Pennyworth Kennel, Newington, New Hampshire, owned by Mrs. Margaret Newcombe.

Stoney Meadows

Stoney Meadows Kennels, operated by Mrs. W. Potter Wear, quickly became a top breeding and show establishment. Mrs. Wear had her own ideas on developing a blood line and used a heavy program of line breeding to establish foundation brood stock. This system worked well in many cases, producing the outstanding Whippet, Ch. Stoney Meadows Masquerade. Stoney Meadows used a number of well-known American families and then introduced English blood into the breeding program. In recent years this kennel has bred within its own families with limited additions of outside American bloodlines. Mrs. Wear developed a type within the breed that distinguished the appearance of Stoney Meadows Whippets as compared to many other types seen in the show ring. Many are similar in type to Meander Whippets. Stoney Meadows Whippets appear in many American pedigrees, and the kennel remains competitively active in the show ring at this writing.

Pennyworth

Pennyworth Kennels was the first registered with the American Kennel Club in 1940, while Margaret Newcombe, then unmarried, was managing Clairedale Kennels for her mother, Mrs. Claire K. Dixon. Mrs. Newcombe first became interested in Whippets after talking with Mrs. George Anderson. Love of the Whippet was instant with Peggy Newcombe, resulting in the purchase of Ch. Carefree and Ch. Sunny Jim of Mardomere. The following years read much like a fairy tale, as Pennyworth, operating much like Mardomere with both homebred and purchased English-type

Whippets, set brilliant records in the show ring all across America. Pennyworth Kennels reached its peak of perfection while operating from Newington, New Hampshire.

Other Important Fanciers

Christine Young, now married to Richard Cormany continued her activities in Whippets. Her first prefix was Corsian, but was later changed to Strathoak when the American Kennel Club disallowed the name Corsian. Two of her best-known Whippets during the period were Ch. Corsian Sunbrilliant and Silhouette. Incidentally, Christine Young registered her first litter in 1937, and both of us on occasions carried the American Whippet Club column in the *American Kennel Gazette* during the 1930s. Betty West, whose family had been active in Whippets on Long Island since the 1920s, married Philip Fell. It was to be a few years before her Badgewood Kennels would hold a prominent place in English and American Whippet activities. Mrs. Wendell Howell, Great Circle Kennels, California, had owned Whippets since childhood. It was in the 1950s that the Whippet bug really took hold of Wendy, and she became an important figure in racing and showing in all sections of the United States. Canyon Crest Kennels, owned by Mrs. W. O. Bagshaw, Beverly Hills, California, was for many years the leading Whippet kennel in California. Canyon Crest Whippets, handled by professional handler, Harry Sangster, became known all over the United States, but greatest success was along the Pacific Coast. Canyon Crest Whippets were mostly on the small side resembling the type most popular in England. Gertrude Hoof, a close friend of Julia Shearer, was also active in the California Whippet Fancy, exhibiting mostly the larger dogs typical of Meander type. Donald Hostetter, Lazeland Kennels, was soon to move from California to Virginia to become one of our most respected breeders of the multiple-purpose Whippet. Marion Woodcock, who helped introduce Whippet racing in California in the 1920s continued her activities in the show ring. Harry Peters, Sr., and Jr., owners of the Windholme Kennels, Islip, New York, both had been active in the American Whippet Club since the 1930s. Harry Peters, Jr. now began showing larger numbers of Windholme-owned dogs at American Whippet Club specialties and the larger all-breed shows in the Eastern section of the United States. Gene and Sibyl Jacobs, Whipoo Kennels, Mahomet, Illinois, were starting their kennel which was to become one of the most successful in the Midwest. Whipoo bred from one to five litters each year and produced many champions. Whipoo bred for show and racing but was superior in the show ring. Ch. Whipoo's Whimsy, CD, was the most versatile dog bred by Whipoo. Ch. Whipoo's

Ch. Picardia Fieldfare and his get at the 1953 AWC Specialty. Julia Shearer is shown with Fieldfare on the extreme left. Other handlers (from left) are Harry Peters, Jr., Agnes Griswold, Peggy Newcombe, Harry Bridges, and Judith Shearer. The others are unidentified. *Shafer*

Ch. Answer of Meander (right), owned and handled by Jeanne Millett, and Lady Penelope of Dundalk, owned by L. S. Reisinger, were WD and WB at the 1951 AWC Specialty under Alva Rosenberg. Answer finished his championship here and Penelope was BW. *Shafer.*

Tar Heel was the dam of 13 champions and was probably their best producing brood bitch.

Focus on the Show Ring

All-breed, unbenched shows were now on the increase in all sections of the United States. Communications and transportation were greatly improved. Whippet entries at shows were still very small, and registrations with the American Kennel Club were few in number as compared to many other breeds. The greatest progress made during the non-physical period of the Whippet in America was that the breed was beginning to move from an Eastern-controlled American Whippet Club to a breed club that was of a truly national character.

Unregistered purebred dogs could still be shown in AKC shows as *listed* for a small, additional fee, generally 25¢. Catalogs still varied greatly in listing breeds, classes and other essential information. Sale price was often posted beside the name of an entry.

In 1930, at the Long Beach Kennel Club (California), judge Sinnot gave BB to Tod Ford's Arroyo Calpha. Well-known exhibitors of the period were Chris Shuttleworth, George Gayton and Freeman Ford. At Westminster that year T. Dickson Smith awarded BB to Nora of Sion Hill, owned by Althea Kennels, over 22 entries and the BB winner at the Eastern Dog Club (Massachusetts) for 1930 was Joseph P. Day's Patricia of Sion Hill.

In 1935 Joseph Batten judged Westminster and found his BB in Meander Kennels' Sandburnette of Meander. At Eastern, Coquette von Burgfried won the breed. Active breeder-exhibitors of the day included Meander Kennels, William A. Short, Mrs. Sherman P. Haight, Elizabeth A. Reimer, Windholme Kennels and William J. Kelly.

As the new decade commenced, a breed entry of 24 was on hand at the Maryland show. Alva Rosenberg judged and awarded BB to Ch. Mirror of Meander with BOS to Ch. Nimbus of Meander, both were owned by Meander Kennels. At Westminster that year Ch. Pegram's Red Wagon was BB and went on to place third in the Hound Group.

Five years later Alva Rosenberg judged the breed again at Maryland. His choices for BB and BOS were Nightshade of Meander over an entry of 40 and Ch. Meander Meteor, respectively. Quentin Twatchman officiated at Westminster in 1945, finding Ch. White Iris of Mardomere his BB and Ch. Ptarmigan of Meander BOS. There were 14 dogs present.

At mid-century Strathoak Star Bid, owned by Mrs. William Powell, was best Whippet at Beverly-Riviera, while at Westminster Harry Peters, Jr. sent Ch. Stoney Meadows Masquerade, owned by Mrs. W. Potter Wear, to the top spot, and made Ch. Rhythm of Mardomere BOS. At

Maryland Carroll Steward, Jr. chose Mrs. John A. Griswold's Ch. Canistone Cayenne BB. At Eastern, Jerry Collins gave the breed to Ch. Stoney Meadows Masquerade.

In 1955, the best Whippet at the Western Reserve Kennel Club (Ohio) was Whipoo's Brushburn, owned by Mrs. Eugene Jacobs. At Maryland it was Ch. Meander Kingfisher who took the breed in an entry of nine under James W. Trullinger. At Orange Empire (California), Ch. Canyon Crest Mamie, from the Canyon Crest establishment, was best while at the Ladies Kennel Association of America show on Long Island Ch. Starglow of Mardomere prevailed in an entry of six under Mr. Trullinger.

At Westminster in 1955, Mrs. Cyril Pacey of England carried Pennyworth Kennels' Ch. Wingedfoot Fieldspring Bryony to BB with BOS to Ch. Canyon Crest Teardrop, from Canyon Crest Kennels. At the 1955 edition of the Eastern Dog Club show Stoney Meadows Kennels took the breed under Dr. A. A. Mitten with Ch. Stoney Meadows By-Line in an entry of 14.

A spot check of Whippets registered with The American Kennel Club during the period 1930 through 1955 clearly indicates the lack of interest in owning registered stock: 1930—54; 1940—77; 1950—89 and 1955—146. It was very easy to see that you could be a very big factor in the show ring with very little competition.

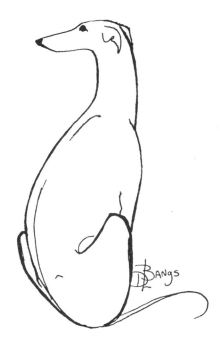

Ch. Laguna Lucky Lad (Ch. Laguna Liege ex Ch. Brekin Ballet Shoes),—owned by Mardomere Kennels and bred by Mrs. D. U. McKay. This fawn and white English import was one of the most successful of the breed in America. He was a good producer and a multiple BIS winner. He was also the first Whippet to win the Hound Group at Westminster. He is shown here winning the Group at the Union County Kennel Club under Sara Peterman, Harry Murphy handling.

Shafer

4

The Whippet from 1956 through 1964

THE SINGLE most important happening for the breed in 1956 was the establishment of the *Whippet News*. It was brought into being to develop a network of communication among all American fanciers and to promote greater understanding of all phases of Whippet activity. Over the years the *Whippet News* was to become a vital source of news, information and ideas. Numerous articles on a wide variety of important subjects appeared in it and contributors represented a broad cross-section of show fanciers, racing enthusiasts, breeders, the historically-minded and many others.

Louis Pegram was the first editor for the new venture. That the *Whippet News* succeeded in its purpose will be seen as the years are reviewed in this and the next chapter.

In this year the American Whippet Club voted to have three Specialty shows per year; one Eastern, one Midwestern and one on the West Coast. There was considerable support for equal status given to all Specialties. It was the decision of the then-current AWC Board that Midwestern and West Coast groups would have to support their own affairs. The Eastern Specialty would be treated as it had been in previous years and so had the distinction of still being "the Whippet Specialty."

The Whippet was at the threshhold of an unprecedented period of growth.

An increase in show entries was noted during this year. Writing in the *Whippet News*, Dr. Samuel H. Scott noted that 249 all-breed shows had Whippet entries. Five dogs had a total of 10 BIS between them. These were Ch. Canyon Crest Mamie, Ch. Canyon Crest Teardrop, Ch. Canyon Crest Jet Princess, Ch. Laguna Lucky Lad and Ch. Meander Mazurka. Twelve dogs had won 41 Hound Groups between them and 14 had 40 Group seconds.

Some of the important winners of 1957 were Ch. Great Circle Holiday, Ch. Meander Bobwhite, Ch. Stoney Meadows Sport Extra, Ch. Stoney Meadows Snow Queen, Ch. Whipoo's Wild Honey, Ch. Wingedfoot Fieldspring Bryony, Ch. Stoney Meadows Monocle, Ch. Pennyworth Impression, Ch. Fascination of Mardomere, Ch. Whipoo's Whimsey, CD, Ch. Great Circle Hester, Ch. Mighty Mouse of Garden City, Ch. Pennyworth Impressive and Ch. Picardi Pollyanna.

Mrs. W. Potter Wear judged the breed at Westminster, awarding BB to Ch. Fascination of Mardomere and BOS to Ch. Meander Bobwhite. The American fancy had an important visitor in the person of Mr. C. H. Douglas Todd. Mr. Todd, a famous British authority, is best-known for his Wingedfoot prefix and wrote *The Popular Whippet*. During this trip, Mr. Todd judged Whippets at the Eastern Dog Club show. Thinking to satisfy what would seem an English judge's natural preference, most exhibitors brought Mr. Todd their smaller dogs. Size, however, did not seem a deciding factor with him, and his BB was Mrs. Wendell Howell's Ch. Great Circle Holiday, a dog of completely American type.

The author had the pleasure of visiting with Douglas Todd during the latter's American visit. He proved to be excellent company and very knowledgeable of the breed in the show ring. He was, however, not as keen on the racing side of the picture.

For the first time since 1948 interest in Whippet racing was revived. Through the efforts of Mrs. Wendell Howell the Northern California Whippet Racing Association came into being. Not content with igniting a spark in the West only, Mrs. Howell, with dogs and racing gear in tow, drove from San Francisco to Illinois to enlist the aid of Sibyl and Eugene Jacobs in Whippet racing. As a result of Mrs. Howell's visit the Jacobses formed the Central States Racing Association.

Mrs. Howell's racing equipment was modeled after the equipment used during the mid 1920s and early 1930s. Its design was obsolete, but the untiring enthusiasm shown by this dedicated fancier rekindled the interest in Whippet racing. Before long the "new-old" sport was gaining friends across the entire United States.

This was the year in which four Milwaukee, Wisconsin fanciers began what were to become successful runs with the breed. They were Ralph

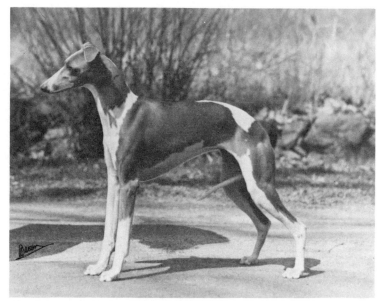

Ch. Pennyworth Blue Iris (Ch. Seagift Penniesworth ex Impressive of Mardomere), owned and bred by Margaret Newcombe, was the first homebred BIS winner for Pennyworth Kennels. This bitch was also an excellent producer. *Brown*

Ch. Wingedfoot Fieldspring Bryony, owned by Margaret New-combe, was an English champion prior to importation and became a Hound Group winner in the United States. *Brown*

and Barbara Eyles (Eyleland) and Barbara and Josephine Steinberg (Traymatt). Both Eyleland and Traymatt were to take places of major importance in the show ring and on the race track.

During 1957 a total of 160 Whippets were registered by the American Kennel Club.

1958

This was a year marked by a continued upswing in the show ring, on the race track and in the breeding paddock. Whippets were beginning to make their move in earnest.

Eugene Jacobs became editor of the *Whippet News,* official publication of the American Whippet Club, and there was an exciting, new development on the racing side of the picture.

Mrs. Wendell Howell, working with Mrs. C. Groverman Ellis, President of the International Kennel Club of Chicago, and William Ogilvie, made arrangements for exhibition Whippet races to be held in conjunction with the Club's annual all-breed show. This was the first time Whippet racing was featured as an added attraction since the old Morris and Essex shows of the mid 1940s and afforded a golden opportunity to introduce the sport to legions of new followers.

A dirt track, 150 yards long, was laid out over part of the International Amphitheater floor. There were 16 starters for these races and the final winner was Ch. Whipoo's Whimsey, CD. It was appropriate that the ultimate winner here was also a conformation champion and a titled obedience dog, as it proved to all how really versatile the Whippet can be.

Dogs came from many places to participate in the first Chicago International race meeting. Some were flown in from Mrs. Howell's kennels in San Francisco while others came from various parts of the Midwest. The winner was local, owned by Mr. and Mrs. E. B. Hopkins of Champaign, Illinois.

The author was Racing Secretary on this historic occasion while members of the Central States Racing Association operated the starting box and lure. This marked the beginning of featured Whippet races as an integral part of many important show gatherings over the coming years.

Ch. Laguna Lucky Lad made breed history in 1958 by winning the Hound Group at Westminster; a first for the breed. He was handled to this great win by Harry Murphy. At Philadelphia Ch. Meander Mockingbird won BB over a large entry under the late Alva Rosenberg. Mockingbird was, in the author's opinion, a most beautiful and feminine example of the breed. Unfortunately, lack of animation in competition caused her problems on various occasions.

The Western AWC Specialty had an entry of 35 in 1958. Mrs. Marion

A scene from the first race meeting held with the International Kennel Club (Chicago). The starting box shown here has been improved upon in the intervening years to make for better racing. The starter was Red Bailey. *Frasie*

Whippets breaking from a Greyhound starting box at the Mutanomah Greyhound Track in Fairview, Oregon. The prime movers for Whippet racing in the Pacific Northwest were members of the Robert Baumgartner family. *Taylorcraft*

Woodcock judged and made Ch. Canyon Crest Jet Lady BB. There were other important developments in the West during this year. John R. Hutchins imported the outstanding brindle winner Ch. Fleeting Falcon for his Briarwyn Kennels in San Antonio, Texas. This dog was one of the outstanding dogs in England prior to his expatriation. He continued his winning ways in his new country, accounting for six BIS and shone as a sire with 14 champion get.

The West also scored some gains in racing at this time. Pearl and Bob Baumgartner, owners of White Acres Kennels, together with their daughter Carol, brought about the revival of interest in Whippet racing in the Pacific Northwest. This part of the country had been an important center of Whippet racing during the 1920s. The first official race meeting was held by the Puget Sound Kennel Club on July 17, 1926 in Seattle, Washington. The Baumgartners got racing going for Whippets on the flat, 200-yard track and also at the Multanomah Greyhound Track in Portland, Oregon.

In England that year the National Whippet Association had 233 entries at its Specialty show. Winner of the dog C.C. was T.E. Jones' Ch. Robmaywin Stargazer of Allways with the bitch C.C. going to Mrs. D. U. McKay's Ch. Lily of Laguna. At the Northern Counties Whippet Club open show, BB in an entry of 46 was Miss Penny Lov, owned by Mrs. Blackburn.

Two Whippets scored American BIS wins during 1958, but both were English imports. Ch. Fleeting Flacon had six BIS as mentioned before and Ch. Laguna Lucky Lad had four. Ten dogs won 46 GR1s, 14 had 38 GR2s and 22 had 40 GR3s between them.

This was a year of many beginnings for fanciers who would achieve the front rank of fame in the Whippet fancy. Donald Hostetter established his Lazeland Kennels at Cobham, Virginia after moving East from California. Robert Motch was building his Seven League establishment through his good brood bitches, and Harry Bridges gave his name and his talent to his Harbridge Whippets operating out of Lansing, Michigan. The Harbridges strongly favored the smaller, English type and are behind many of today's top-producing families.

In the obedience ring, Picardia Priscilla, owned by Donald Frames, became the first Whippet to earn the Utility degree.

A noteworthy increase in registrations took place in 1958 with a total of 232 registered by the American Kennel Club.

1959

This was a year of improved communication and growth in the Whippet fancy from coast to coast. The *Whippet News* as the official organ for

Ch. Fleeting Falcon (Fleeting Father O'Flynn ex Fleeting Oldown Snipe), owned by Margaret Newcombe and bred by Mrs. M. B. Garrish. This solid brindle import was a strong sire and multiple BIS winner. He is shown being awarded the last of his eight BIS at the North Shore Kennel Club under Hayes Blake Hoyt, Mrs. Newcombe handling.

the breed encouraged positive growth, and it appeared that fanciers were seriously thinking of the Whippet as a true, multiple-purpose animal: show dog, racer and superior pet.

The 1959 show season began at Westminster. Judge Mrs. Statter Day gave BB, in an entry of 28, to Ch. Laguna Lucky Lad, owned by Mardomere Kennels and BOS to Mrs. Wendell Howell's Ch. Great Circle Holiday. At the Eastern Dog Club show, Kenneth Given placed Ch. Stoney Meadows Snow Queen BB with Donald Hostetter's Liebeskind O'Lazeland BOS.

Whippets at the Maryland Kennel Club were judged by Mrs. W. Potter Wear. She selected Ch. Meander Mockingbird for BB and Mrs. Howell's Ch. Wingedfoot Domenic for BOS. At Saw Mill River Mrs. Philip Fell gave the breed to Lucky Dream of Mardomere and BOS to Liebeskind O'Lazeland.

In the Midwest, Alva Rosenberg passed on 32 Whippets at International. He awarded BB to Ch. Great Circle Hester, owned by Ralph and Barbara Eyles, and BOS to Mrs. Howell's Ch. Great Circle The Scot. The Western Parent Specialty was held with the Del Monte Kennel Club show in Pebble Beach, California. Thirty-two Whippets came forward for judge Donald Hostetter who awarded the purple-and-gold to Ch. Great Circle Holiday. The Eastern Parent Specialty that year was judged by William W. Brainard, Jr. Fifty Whippets in 87 entries were on hand for the event, and Ch. Meander Mockingbird was named the best one. Mr. Brainard's choice for BOS was Ch. Liebeskind O'Lazeland.

Some of the other important shows of 1959 include the Ladies' Kennel Association show where Mrs. Geraldine R. Dodge sent Ch. Laguna Lucky Lad into the Hound Group and the North Shore (Mass.) show where Percy Roberts picked Ch. Fleeting Falcon for BB in an entry of 18 Whippets.

Whippets were well represented on the 1959 New England circuit with Ch. Seven League Saddler, owned by Bobby Motch; taking the breed at the Rockingham and Lakes Region shows, Ch. Fleeting Falcon was best Whippet at Caroll County and Green Mountain with Mrs. Wear's Stoney Meadows Red Fox topping the field at Champlain Valley.

Notable results of early autumn shows include a BB win at Westbury for Ch. Laguna Lucky Lad and a clean sweep of the top awards at Devon by Whipoo Kennels. In a field of 17, Ch. Whippo's Spaterib of Meander was BB and Whipoo's White Luster was BOS.

In England 62 Whippets turned out at Manchester. Best of Breed and Best Hound was G. Manning's Oldoaks White Rajah. The Championship show of the Northern Counties Whippet Club drew 89 dogs for American judge Anton Rost. His choice for the top spot was Ch. Robmaywin Stargazer of Allways, owned by F. E. Jones. Later in the year, at the same club, A. Hudson's Cockrow Winter Jasmine was Best in Specialty.

Interest in the Whippet was steadily increasing by the close of the decade. This growth was not limited to the show ring as we will soon see. Whippet racing was gaining back much of its old popularity and all over the country fanciers were sparing no effort to promote the breed and help newcomers along.

A factor of key importance in breed growth was the *Whippet News*. In every sense it was an organ for distributing information to all Whippet people. Articles by highly respected personalities in the breed were always being offered. They were articles covering every conceivable topic of interest from the practical matters of feeding and kenneling dogs to reports of activities and travels of individuals and everything in between. It was indeed fortunate that the *Whippet News* came into being when it would be needed most. Its value to the entire fancy can never be overestimated.

The Chicago International race meeting continued as the most important Whippet racing event of the year. Barbara and Ralph Eyles donated three impressive trophies to be used as perpetual awards for this annual meeting. These trophies, by their inclusion, added prestige and dignity to Whippet racing.

Top racer at the 1959 meet was again Ch. Whipoo's Whimsey, CD, repeating the win of the previous year. Second was Mrs. Wendell Howell's import, Ch. Wingedfoot Domenic, a 20-pound speedster who, in the author's opinion, was the fastest small Whippet ever to race in America. There were 15 starters for the meet.

Dogs under a year old raced in the puppy division with Eyleland Peppermint Boy and Eyleland Stoney Meadows Tost finishing first and second respectively.

An important ingredient in the growth of Whippet racing at this time was the number of opportunities available for schooling and racing dogs under actual track conditions. The Central States Racing Association, the Oklahoma Whippet Club, the Northern California Racing Club and several other groups held exhibition races, schooling races and training programs. Donald Hostetter arranged for informal races to be held in conjunction with the 1959 AWC Eastern Specialty show.

It is encouraging to note that a significant number of the top racing Whippets of 1959 were also conformation champions, indicating interest in both racing and showing by the same fanciers.

In 1959 Ch. Fleeting Falcon was purchased from John Hutchins by Peggy Newcombe for her Pennyworth Kennels. The year also found Calvin Perry getting started in the breed, and it marked the retirement of Ch. Great Circle Holiday from the show ring. This bitch was a BIS winner as well as a Specialty winner and a major threat at any race meeting.

Registrations showed a slight decrease for 1959 with 226 individuals registered by the American Kennel Club.

71

1960

The Whippet continued to make steady gains at this time, helped by a healthy, sporting outlook held by the majority of most fanciers. Breeding programs were going forward and many kennels were in the happy position of having no shortage of good young stock for themselves and for the use of newcomers to the breed.

A large kennel must have an active breeding program to enable a steady flow of new dogs to enter the show ring. As a result, many of the puppies not needed came into the hands of people starting on their way. It will be seen that the new fanciers derived great benefit from this readily-available pool of well-bred puppies.

The single, most important dog show event of 1960 was the AWC Eastern Specialty. The show was held at the home of Mr. and Mrs. W. Potter Wear in Pennllyn, Pennsylvania, and attracted fanciers from every part of the United States. The entry of 86 was made by 58 dogs. Mrs. Theodore Pedersen judged puppy sweepstakes and the all-breed judge Winifred Heckmann officiated in the regular classes, finding her BB winner in Calvin G. Perry's Ch. Stoney Meadows Sprint.

Whippet racing appeared on the program for this Specialty as an extra added attraction. Eastern racing enthusiasts under the direction of Donald Hostetter set up a 200-yard turf track. This group constructed and used a new-type starting box modeled on the starting boxes used by most American Greyhound tracks. The new box proved very satisfactory, far superior to those in current use and was soon adopted by race groups all over the country. The winner of the Specialty race meeting was Eyleland Peppermint Boy (Eyles). Ch. Meander Flip the Dip and Meander Ten Four finished second and fourth high point racers. It was the only time the author can recall Meander Kennels racing its own dogs.

At Westminster Mrs. Philip Fell selected Ch. Stoney Meadows Snow Queen for BB and at International the late George Beckett conferred the same honor on Mrs. Robert Henderson's Ch. Great Circle Mad Hatter.

The International race meeting of 1960 brought out 14 adult starters with ultimate victory going to the previous year's runner-up Ch. Wingedfoot Domenic. Eyleland Peppermint Boy took down second honors this day.

Later in the year Domenic showed himself more than equal to moving from track to show ring and winning well in either department. It was on the occasion of the AWC Western Specialty show. The renowned English all-breed authority Leo C. Wilson was judging as part of his first judging trip to America, and Domenic successfully annexed the breed.

Mrs. Wendell Howell was very active with the Northern California Whippet Association in this year. However, she found time for a trip to Holland to study the Dutch racing practices. There is a circular track near

Amsterdam which she was particularly keen to see. Her trip revealed that the Dutch and Germans have less racing than the English, but we have been able to secure better information from them, particularly on circular track racing for all sight hounds. It is interesting to note that the Dutch use a motorcycle to drag the lure around the track to arouse the interest of the dogs racing.

A new race course was established in 1960 at the home of Mrs. Robert Henderson in Hillsboro, California. Also in 1960 Joyce Anson of Aldergrove, British Columbia organized a racing club in her area. Mrs. Anson was experienced with racing Greyhounds in England and ultimately took an active part in showing Whippets in the United States and Canada.

In spite of the active interest in breeding and promoting Whippets at this time, only 184 Whippets were registered by the American Kennel Club during 1960.

1961

Competition in the Whippet ring was on the increase in 1961. Many exhibitors in search of larger entries and good competition went out of their home areas to show. This was particularly true among Midwestern fanciers who swelled the entries at major Eastern shows.

Whippet entries at many California shows were also growing at this time. Joyce Anson was bringing dogs from British Columbia and the Baumgartners were doing the same from the State of Washington. It all served as a spur to larger entries in the Golden State.

Breeding activity was also notably brisk with both large and small kennels doing their part. It was fairly common for the larger kennels to buy or even trade puppies and grown dogs among each other. This was usually done to acquire a good show prospect rather than to bring in a new breeding line.

The Eastern Specialty was again held at the Wears' Stoney Meadows farm and brought together a brilliant collection of Whippets for the respected opinion of James A. Farrell, Jr. Best of Breed in a sizzling field of 89 competitors was Ch. Renpark's Jeff of Sheldegren, owned by Janet C. Koch.

As in the previous year, exhibition racing was the extra attraction. The winner was a repeat of the year before in Eyleland Peppermint Boy.

The Western Specialty was held with the beautiful Santa Barbara show. The winner here was Mrs. Cormany's Ch. Strathoak Starsheen under Margaret Newcombe. Other important show results of the year include Westminster where Ch. Laguna Lucky Lad was BB in an entry of 20 under Gen. E. B. McKinley; Maryland at which Ch. Meander Wet Paint took the breed for owner Bobby Motch with 19 in competition.

The AWC also staged a Specialty in New England, at North Conway, New Hampshire. Judge Donald Hostetter selected Ch. Eyeland Winter Wind, owned by Barbara and Ralph Eyles for BB. She went on to win the Hound Group this day under Alva Rosenberg. Donald Hostetter also judged a large, supported entry at Champaign, Illinois. His choice here was Traymatt Kennels' Traymatt Eyeland Herkimer.

The results of the International in 1961 furnished a valuable object lesson for all fanciers concerning breeding dogs for their original purpose.

The BB winner, under Harry T. Peters, Jr., was Eyeland Kennels' Eyeland Red Mack, a litter brother to the peerless track star, Peppermint Boy. And, to put the icing on the cake, Peppermint Boy was high point winner for the race meeting. Moral of the story—a show dog can do what it was bred for. The second highpoint racer was Dr. H . W. Heiser's Tubara's Choir Boy.

In England, the Crufts show drew 142 Whippets in 239 entries for the veteran breeder-judge Mrs. C. A. "Poppy" Martin who awarded BB to the Specialty-winning Ch. Teighways Tasmin, owned by Fred Barnes.

Racing was now well-established in many parts of the United States and many of the outstanding racing Whippets of the day were also winners in the conformation ring. The International show and race meeting proved that good race dogs and good show dogs can come from the same family and even the same litter. It is an everlasting credit to the breed that this dual nature exists in the Whippet. The AWC succeeded in encouraging and promoting the multiple purpose Whippet.

For the most part those whose dogs competed in the show ring took an active part in Whippet racing as well. The breed was yet to feel the impact of those whose major, long-term interest was in racing only.

It was in 1961 that Mrs. Wendell Howell, of the Great Circle Whippets, removed to Ireland. Her loss to the American fancy was most keenly felt, as was her vigorous promotion of racing and her many views published in the *Whippet News* . It was through the *Whippet News* that Americans and Mrs. Howell kept in touch. Indeed, many of her experiences and activities in her new home could easily fill a book by themselves.

Mrs. Howell's good winner Ch. Wingedfield Domenic suffered no setback by crossing an ocean and proved it by winning the Dutch National Championship on the famous Amsterdam track. In America he was able to hold his own against larger dogs, so prevailed easily over the Dutch competition which was closer to his own size and type.

C.H. Douglas Todd's *The Popular Whippet* was published in 1961 and was available to American fanciers. While primarily written for the British fancy, it offered a good deal of useful information for anyone interested in the breed, regardless of citizenship.

Only three dogs registered BIS wins in 1961. Ch. Bull O'The Woods

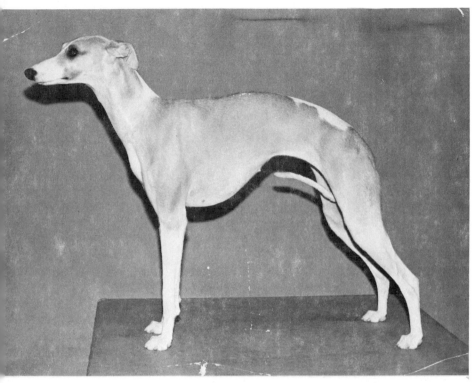

. Selbrook Highlight (Robmaywin Stargazer of Allways ex Porthurst Creme de Men-
), owned by Mrs. Clare C. Hodge and bred by Mesdames J. and D. Selby (England). A
nner of three BIS and the dam of nine champions, she was the foundation matron of
s. Hodge's Highlight Kennels. *Rost*

O'Blue Beaver had twice gone the whole way with Ch. Fleeting Falcon and Ch. Selbrook Highlight gathering one supreme award each.

The general decline in registrations of the past two years was now dramatically reversed with 262 dogs added to the rolls in 1961. The increase in breeding activity was starting to be reflected in the American Kennel Club records.

1962

The growth trend in the breed continued in 1962 and the fancy was steadfast in its support and promotion. The real development of the dual-purpose Whippet was evident by this time and the AWC was steadily growing into a national organization. Registrations were dramatically up with a 42% increase in 1961 over the total of the previous year. The 262 Whippets registered by AKC in 1961 were still a far cry from the 1,951 Kennel Club (England) registrations for the same year.

As with any growing organization, the AWC was experiencing the effects of growing pains. In a rapidly changing world, many older, established Club members, feeling deep pride in past and present accomplishments, held views differing from those of the newer fanciers. Quite naturally, conflicts stemming from differing philosophies were bound to arise. But when major issues developed, newcomers, who often owned foundation stock bred by the older and larger kennels, sided with their mentors in the political affairs of the AWC.

Since the mid 1950s the prevailing attitude in the Whippet fancy had been to operate in the best interests of the breed. Unfortunately this was now starting to change, with some Club members showing more interest in their own positions and quest for prestige than what best served the Whippet breed. If not for the positive direction of the Club's growth during the previous eight years the breed might have suffered some very severe setbacks.

This was also a year of change for the *Whippet News*. Up to now the *Whippet News* had concentrated on printing articles of interest to all that were useful to many and as unbiased as possible. Unfortunately, controversial letters began appearing in print in the Club organ, letters written by status seekers who were trying to undermine their rivals. Sad too is the fact that such smear tactics were effective, and the cooperative spirit so long a part of the Whippet fancy faded accordingly.

In spite of the "pot-shots in print" the *Whippet News* was selected as the best breed bulletin from the Hound Group and won the *Dog World* trophy for 1962. The judging was based on editorial content and applicability of the material to both the novice and the breeder.

In the show ring the most important event continued to be the Eastern

76

Mr. R. Kornblith accepting a trophy from Mrs. C. G. Ellis and Donald Hostetter for the performance of his Ch. Eyleland Peppermint Boy at the 1962 International race meeting.

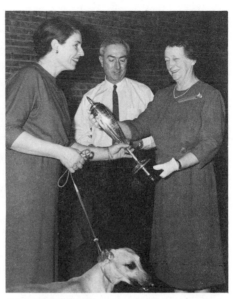

Mrs. Ralph Eyles accepts the trophy for the achievements of Ch. Eyleland Cinnamon Roll from Mrs. Ellis and Mr. Hostetter.

Mrs. Ellis and Mr. Hostetter present the trophy for high point puppy racer to Victor Renner.

James Martinez and Ch. Briarwyn's Blue Stone were also in the winners' circle at the International races with Mrs. Ellis and Mr. Hostetter in 1962.

AWC Specialty. This year there was a change of venue and the show was held in Keswick, Virginia. Judith Shearer presided over the Puppy Futurity and gave first to Whipoo Kennels' Twist of Lemon, bred by the author. Harry T. Peters, Jr. was the judge of the regular classes and placed Mrs. W. P. Wear's Stoney Meadows Hell's Bells BB.

This year the races in connection with the Specialty were held the day before at Donald Hostetter's Pagebrook Downs farm in Cobham, Virginia. A 250-yard track was laid out for the occasion and no fewer than 45 starters took part in the event. Ch. Eyleland Cinnamon Roll took top honors in a "squeaker" with Ch. Rouget O'Lazeland second. High point puppy was Petite (Renner/Berger).

When all the show results for the year were tabulated Ch. Selbrook Highlight, owned by Mrs. Clare C. Hodge, was the year's top winner with a record of 12 GR1s, 9 GR2s, 6 GR3s and 2 GR4s. Ch. Bull O'The Woods O'Blue Beaver and Ch. Seven League Songbird each had one BIS during the year.

The Midwest Parent Specialty, held in Chicago, brought out 58 dogs for Julia Shearer. Her choice for Best of Breed was Ch. Eyleland Winter Wind. By now the races were a fixture at Chicago, and this year a record entry of 36 adult and 10 puppy starters turned out. Tied for high point honors were Eyleland Peppermint Boy (Kornblith) and Ch. Eyleland Cinnamon Roll (Eyles), and third was Briarwyn's Blue Stone (Martinez). A portable starting box was in use at this race that was built by Ralph Eyles following the design of those in use at Eastern race meetings.

Ch. Seven League Songbird was BB at the New England AWC Specialty for owner Bobby Motch while Just Richard took the breed at Champaign, Illinois in a supported entry under Judith Shearer and later took a GR2 for owner Louis Pegram. On the West Coast Donald Hostetter gave Ch. Eyleland Winter Wind her second Specialty BB in a year in an entry of 49 Whippets.

In 1962 a business transaction concerning the sale and importation of a dog took place which was to have profound implications for the breed. The agent for the buyer was Mrs. Martine Collings, the buyer was Peggy Newcombe and the dog was a young son of Bellavista Barry out of Myhorlyns Anita, bred by A. E. Halliwell. His name—Courtenay Fleetfoot.

Whippet registrations continued to rise with 287 dogs registered by the American Kennel Club in 1962.

1963

There could be little doubt that by the beginning of 1963 the Whippet was demanding, and getting, an ever-more important place in the world of

Ch. Stoney Meadows Hell's Bells made a striking win enroute
to his title by annexing BB at the 1962 AWC Specialty under
judge Harry T. Peters, Jr. This owner-handled homebred
came form the senior puppy class to score this spectaular win
for the Potter Wears.   *Shafer*

At the Eastern Dog Club show (Boston), 1962 a well-matched
team of blue Whippets was Best Team in Show under James
A. Farrell, Jr. This talented quartet was owned and handled by
Janet Koch and Joan Bartlett.   *Brown*

purebred dogs. Growth within the breed was vigorous, but with it came the inevitable growing pains. There was a changing way of life in general and it was felt in the Whippet fancy. Many self-interests came into play and many loud voices were heard. Clashes between personalities stemming from ambition were all too common during this year in the Whippet fancy.

Westminster was, as usual, the first important event of the new year. Donald Hostetter had the judging duties and sent Ch. Eyeland Winter Wind into the Hound Group. The Midwest AWC Specialty was held in Chicago, the day before International. Here Alva Rosenberg seconded Mr. Hostetter's February decision by awarding Best in Specialty to Winter Wind for yet a third Specialty best. Stoney Meadows Beauty Queen was BW at the Specialty, and the next day at International she repeated the win and went on to BB under William W. Brainard, Jr.

The race meeting held with International drew 76 adults and 23 puppies; sound proof of this feature's popularity both with the fancy and the paying gate as a spectator attraction. Ch. Eyeland Cinnamon Roll led the field in adults and Stoney Meadows Nora (Renfield Kennels) prevailed among the puppies.

The beautiful Santa Barbara show was the site of the Western AWC in 1963. William Brainard judged here and selected Ch. Great Circle Skibereen, owned by Norman Ellis, for BB. On the preceeding day, at Ventura breeder-judge Judith R. Shearer chose Jack Towne's Eyeland Double or Nothing for best Whippet.

As with Chicago, Whippet racing was on the program at Santa Barbara. Pamela Arthur, down from British Columbia, had a field day here and accounted for the best racer in both puppy and adult categories. Her Rockabye Brandysnap and Sonna Rockabye Baby were the respective winners.

The Eastern Parent Specialty brought forth the largest Whippet entry of the year. Forty-six dogs were gathered together for this red-letter affair. The puppy Futurity, judged by Mrs. Ralph G. Eyles, went to Stoney Meadows Bold Venture and in the regular classes Mrs. Augustus V. Riggs, IV gave the nod for BB to Windholme Kennels' Eyeland Brown Betty.

The Fall AWC race meeting was held the day before the Eastern Specialty, again at Pagebrook Downs. The field consisted of 27 adult and nine puppy starters. Ch. Eyeland Cinnamon Roll repeated his Chicago triumph as high point racer in the adult division. A tie for second honors occured between Eyeland Homer and Eyeland Hannah. The author acted as Racing Secretary for this meet and was assisted in grading the races by William Schmick.

Two additional important gatherings for the breed took place in St. Louis, Missouri and Champaign, Illinois. In the first, the Mississippi Val-

The littermates shown here represent the greatest producing family of dual purpose Whippets in America. At left is Ch. Rouget O'Lazeland with handler John Berger and at right is Ch. Legend O'Lazeland with Donald Hostetter. Sybil Jacobs (Whipoo) is shown with these outstanding animals.

```
                                                         Ch. Meander Robin
                              Ch. Meander Kingfisher     Ch. Dizzy Blond of Meander
             Ch. Fisherman O'Lazeland
                              Summertan O'Lazeland       Ch. Meander Metallurgist
                                                         Ch. Joktan O'Lazeland
      Royal Coachman O'Lazeland
                              Ch. Son of Flick           Flick of Ups and Downs
                                                         Shu Fly
             Ch. Bo Peep of Birdneck Point
                              Happy Birthday of Kingston Ch. Silver Image
CH. LEGEND O'LAZELAND                                    Pride of Kingston
CH. ROUGET O'LAZELAND
                              Ch. Picardia Fieldfare     Sunnysand O'Lazeland
                                                         Ch. Picardia Polka Dot
             Ch. Meander Robin
                              Scarlet Letter of Meander  Ch. Meander Man of Letters
                                                         Hunter's Moon of Meander
      Lorelei O'Lazeland
                              Ch. Oldown Stormy          Samema Snowflight
                                                         Oldown True Love
             Ch. Dizzy Blond of Meander
                              Question of Meander        Ch. Ptarmigan of Meander
                                                         Windholme Cloudy
```

Ch. Eyleland Winter Wind, BB at Westminster 1963, shown with owner/breeder/handler Barbara Eyles.

The Westminster show is always an important gathering place for the Whippet fancy. Here Judy Shearer and Eugene and Sybil Jacobs display some of the competitors outside the ring.

A break in Westminster proceedings allows time for a visit between Julia Shearer, the author and Sybil Jacobs.

ley show, Whippets were judged by Anton Korbel who placed Westmoreland Charles BW and Ch. Wanderlust O'Lazeland BB.

On this day the Mississippi Valley Club presented its first program of Whippet races. A 133-yard track was laid out. This length allowed a sufficient stopping distance at the end of the race. Eyleland Hanna (Eyles) won top honors among adults while Red Varmint (Pegram) led the puppy starters. There was a special, allowance race on the program and was won by the day's BB, Wanderlust. It was a proud day for owner William Schmick. The AWC-supported entry at Champaign was very large this year. Mrs. W. Potter Wear handled the judging duties and found Humble Acres Snow Cloud her best one. Following the judging, schooling races were held in spite of the rainy afternoon.

As can be determined from the documentation of the year's events already mentioned, racing had become an integral part of AWC functions. There was a steady growth of interest in the Whippet as a racing dog and with it an increase in the number of activities available to those who wished to participate.

A Spring race meeting was now being held at Donald Hostetter's Pagebrook farms. Ch. Eyleland Cinnamon Roll prevailed at the 1963 running. A new group, the Midwest Coursing Club, was formed and gave schooling races for sight hounds on the grounds of Traymatt Kennels. In this year also, Barbara and Ralph Eyles opened their new track, Eyleland Park. The opening was a gala occasion with fanciers attending from all over the country. A good turnout of 43 adult Whippets and 10 puppies was the focal point of the affair. As at so many other race meetings this year Ch. Eyleland Cinnamon Roll set the pace and led the pack over the finish line among the adults with Eyleland Homer and Eyleland Hannah tied for second.

In England, 145 Whippets made up 266 entries at the 1963 Crufts show. Mrs. M. B. Garrish put Samarkand's Greenbrae Tarragon at the top of this large entry. It was a good start too, as this dog went on to be the top Whippet in England for that year. Also in England, Peggy Newcombe wore the judge's badge at the Northern Counties Whippet Club show and drew 144 of Britain's best.

A report by Dr. Sam Scott that appeared in the *Whippet News* offered graphic evidence of how important the breed had become in intervariety competition. The report follows:

Whippet Show Activities	1959	1963
All-Breed Shows	450	467
Shows with Whippet entry (%)	58%	81%
Whippet BIS	0	15
Group 1	20	56
Group 2	23	53
Group 3	17	44

The dramatic increase in G1s and BIS can be largely attributed to Ch. Courtenay Fleet-foot of Pennyworth. His 1963 record included 10 BIS and 21 G1s.

The racing side of the picture also scored impressive gains during the year. Racing groups operating in various parts of the country were using virtually the same scoring system to grade dogs and racing equipment was becoming more standardized. The grading system now in use was easily understood by the majority of participants: A-outstanding, B-very good, C-average, D-below average (non-winner).

The most unfortunate happening this year occured in its waning months and concerned the *Whippet News*. The editor and the AWC board locked horns in a disagreement concerning material unsuitable for publication in the official organ of the AWC. It was an altercation that had and still has far-reaching implications in many parts of the Whippet fancy.

The author was directly involved as a Board member and personal friend of all parties. It was a disagreeable situation that, in my opinion, was entirely avoidable. Had the editor taken the time to better understand the Board's decision and the thinking behind it before going to *Whippet News* readers with the cry "censure," the entire matter could have been quietly settled. But this happened when breed rivalries were fierce as never before and many people were unnecessarily involved to the detriment of all. In the end the matter was settled, at least on the surface and the *Whippet News* continued to be published.

The efforts of the AWC and the activities of the fancy in vigorously promoting the Whippet as a versatile companion showed in the registration figures for the year. A total of 399 Whippets were registered with the American Kennel Club during 1963.

1964

In this historical accounting of the Whippet, 1964 must be considered one of the breed's most significant years. Expansion and a growing interest was as evident as in the past. At this point it could not be said that the breed's sphere of influence was limited to one place, or one group or one breeder. The Whippet was now, in every way, a breed of major, national importance.

Fanciers realized early in the year that 1964 would be different. At

Ch. Stoney Meadows Beauty Queen, owned and bred by the
W. Potter Wears, was a strong winner in the 1960s. She is
shown winning the Hound Group at the Ox Ridge Kennel
Club 1964 under Percy Roberts, Mrs. Wear handling.

Shafer.

Sheldegren Whippets were represented at the 1964 Eastern Specialty by (from
left) Sugar Blues with Nathalea Torrey, Prince Johnny with Calvin Perry, Lucky
Penny with Janet Koch and Explorer with Joan Bartlett. *Gilbert.*

Westminster Ch. Courtenay Fleetfoot of Pennyworth was BB and went on to win the Hound Group. He was not finished yet and went all the way to BEST IN SHOW under Judge Len Carey at this, the most prestigious show in America. His Westminster BIS made "Ricky" the first of his breed and only the second Hound in history to make this highly coveted win. Handled throughout his career by Robert Forsyth, this great Whippet proceeded to set a sizzling pace for the remainder of the year. When it was all over he had set a new, all-time record of top wins for the breed, and was the top-winning dog of all breeds for 1964. His wins during this banner year included 21 BIS, Chicago International, Harbor Cities and Ravenna among them and 31 GR1s. He was also BB at the Midwest AWC Specialty.

In subsequent years Ricky would make his strong mark on the breed as a producer—the true measure of a great dog. For now he provided Peggy Newcombe with her most exciting and rewarding year in dogs.

It has already been noted that Ch. Courtenay Fleetfoot of Pennyworth was BB at the Midwest Specialty. The BOS at this affair was another strong winner, Ch. Stoney Meadows Beauty Queen from the kennels of the W. Potter Wears. Beauty Queen subsequently was BB at the AWC Eastern Specialty under Margaret Newcombe, while on the opposite coast Mrs. Wear gave the same award to Mrs. Robert Henderson's Madcap Syndicated News, coming out of the novice class to make this good win.

A look at the show statistics for 1964 reveals that the Whippet was very well represented all over the country. There were entries in 421 of the 488 all-breed shows held that year; over 87.5%. Furthermore, many of the dogs being actively campaigned and winning were of a high level of quality. Fanciers of the Whippet and all other breeds became accustomed to good specimens of the breed being consistently shown.

In British developments, Ch. Samarkand's Greenbrae Tarragon was BB at Crufts for a second time. This win was made over 120 other dogs and preceded a good GR2. Tarragon's 1964 record also included a BB under judge Tovey at the Whippet Club championship show and under Mrs. Blandy at the West of England Ladies' Kennel Society (W.E.L.K.S.). The Northern Counties Whippet Club championship show for 1964 had 129 dogs in 230 entries and the winner here was the 20-month-old Tantivity Diver. More would be heard from this dog following his arrival in America.

England and America were not the only countries where the Whippet star was on the rise. In Sweden, at the 1964 Gothenburg show 42 Whippets were on hand. This was the largest breed entry for this event to date. The breed winner on this day was Bojan Bibbi.

During 1964 47% of all Grade A racers were also AKC champions of record as were 19.5% of the Grade Bs and 8.6% of the Grade Cs. It was

Ch. Courtenay Fleetfoot of Pennyworth (Ch. Bellavista Barry ex Myhorlyns Anita) owned and imported by Margaret P. Newcombe and bred in England by A. E. Halliwell. A great dog and truly a legend in his own time, this phenomenal campaigner had 54 GR1s and 29 BIS including Westminster, Chicago and Harbor Cities in 1964. He was the top-winning dog of all breeds in 1964 and was elected to the *Kennel Review* Hall of Fame in 1972 after four nominations. He had sired well over 50 champions and was the top producing dog of all breeds in 1966. "Ricky" was a champion and a Group winner before coming to America and was probably responsible, in large measure, for the surge of interest in the breed since the days of his campaign.   *Burwell*.

A more informal study of Ch. Courtenay Fleetfoot of Pennyworth as he relaxes among some of the tokens of his triumphant career. He was handled by Robert Forsyth throughout, setting records that have not been matched by another Whippet before or since.

obvious that many winners in the ring were quite capable of doing the breed's work.

In various races held during the year Seven League Something Else and Ch. Eyleland Cinnamon Roll tied for high point honors at Pagebrook Downs' Spring meeting. Victor Renner's Bettebrook Bonita sprinted to high point puppy honors at International while the same owner's Eyleland Homer led the field in the adult feature over 57 starters. Second high point was Ch. Rouget O'Lazeland (Renfield Kennels) and third was Traymatt Rooster Boy (Traymatt Kennels).

For the first time in American Whippet racing, an electric timer was used to clock the contestants. The device, developed by Selwyn Blackstone, gave racing devotees their first real opportunity to accurately time races. The fastest time recorded at International for the 472 feet was 10.26 seconds.

Eyleland Homer and Ch. Rouget O'Lazeland spent a good deal of time crossing finish lines together in 1964. This pair tied for high point at Mississippi Valley and were first and second respectively at the second Eyleland Park meet, reversing the order for the first Central Ohio meet. The latter held a field of 64 starters. Both dogs also travelled to the Santa Barbara meet. Here Homer was second and Rouget third.

At Mississippi Valley Traymatt McArthur and Rooster Boy tied for third and fourth. High point puppy at Central Ohio was John John (Schmick) while at Santa Barbara, Mrs. Lester Babbitt's White Acres Sage won the adult division. Carol Baumgartner's Ch. White Acres Carol's Fancy was high point bitch at Santa Barbara.

Carol's Fancy added further laurels to her racing career by running high point at the first Multanomah race meeting. Ringo's Ringo, owned by the Trounce family was high point puppy. At the second Multanomah meeting the winning adult was Canadian Ch. Gypsy's Kelly, C.D. with Carol's Fancy second. Twenty-one starters were on hand for this one.

In other racing developments the Midwest Coursing Club scheduled monthly schooling races at Eyleland Park. This group, a mixed sight hound club, also offered circular track racing at facilities in Racine, Wisconsin. Fred Cooper, editor of the *Chase News,* built a circular track for mixed sight hound racing at his farm in Northern Illinois. Whippet racing was becoming increasingly more popular in the Pacific Northwest and was being offered as a feature attraction at the Multanomah track in Portland, Oregon. This interest is a direct result of the efforts of the Baumgartner family.

Through the *Whippet News* Mrs. Wendell Howell kept the American fancy informed on many of her activities in Ireland. She wrote that her Ch. Great Circle Bewitched passed away at age 12. Of particular interest was a report from Mrs. Howell concerning her Whippets proving their worth as ratters when the rodents attempted to move into the house at the onset of cooler weather. Her reports of Irish activity in both Whippets and Greyhounds were eagerly awaited and widely read in the United States.

Death claimed three of the breed's staunchest supporters in 1964. The entire American fancy was shocked at the death of Donald Hostetter, AWC President. He was a great friend of the breed and a strong supporter of the Whippet as a dog of many uses. He did as much for the breed in the preceding five-year period as any other fancier in America.

Robert Motch had only been active in the breed for a short while, but his Seven League dogs always gave an excellent account of themselves. His passing was felt keenly in the fancy as was that of John Berger.

John Berger was closely associated with Renfield Kennels and helped the Renners to get their operation going. He was a superior trainer and the achievements of many of the fine racers bearing the Renfield colors could be attributed to him.

The registration curve continued up in 1964 with 429 Whippets being registered with the American Kennel Club.

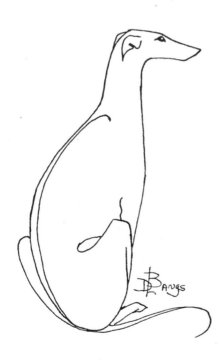

5

The Whippet Since 1965

AFTER the sudden death of Donald Hostetter a number of conspicuous changes affecting the operation of the AWC took place. The three oldest members of the Club resigned from the Board at this time. Life styles in general were undergoing radical changes in America, and the AWC was feeling the pressures of this. Members of the Club disagreed with the Board in matters of policy concerning the operation of the Club. Many newer fanciers were attempting to make a name for themselves in the breed and a place for themselves in AWC affairs. It was a case of old vs. new with the inevitable personality clashes.

Fortunately, the Board, after resignations, was made up of experienced people who had a good background in showing, breeding and racing.

By this time practically anyone interested in the breed could join the AWC. This liberal membership policy quickly proved to have both advantages and disadvantages in Club operations. In 1965 the AWC Constitution and By-Laws were revised following AKC recommendations and guidelines. It was now possible for AWC Board business to be conducted through the mails. Victor Renner became the Club President, bringing to the office a positive combination of good business experience and a commendable string of accomplishments in the breed. So the Whippet continued to make headway in 1965, but was still hampered by those in the fancy who placed personal ambition before breed well-being.

The meteoric show career of Ch. Courtenay Fleetfoot of Pennyworth came to a close with the 1965 Westminster show. Here Ricky was again Best Hound, this time under Anna Katherine Nicholas. His American show record in 87 outings stood at 29 BIS, 54 GR1s, 12 GR2s, 3 GR3s, 2 GR4s and 76 BBs. It was a truly great record for a truly unforgettable dog.

In 1965 Peggy Newcombe added English Ch. Tantivity Diver to her formidable Pennyworth string. Both he and the homebred Pennyworth Burning Dream completed their championships in this year and the power of the just-retired Ricky as a stud was becoming increasingly plainer. He had already sired 12 champions in less than two years.

There was other important show news this year too. The Midwest AWC Specialty took place in Champaign, Illinois. Eugene Jacobs had the honor of judging the entry of 38 and made Ch. Eyleland Cinnamon Roll, owned by Ralph Eyles, his best one. Ch. Madcap Syndicated News was awarded BOS. Her owner, Mrs. Robert Henderson made the long trip from California by auto with Norman Ellis. This is a major undertaking for anyone, but Mrs. Henderson was in her late seventies at the time!

Fanciers at the Midwest Specialty had a chance to see the winning form of Eyleland Hannah as she led the field in exhibition racing. A good turnout the next day was on hand for judge William Schmick. His BB was Norman Ellis' Ch. Madcap Bold Minstrel.

In California the Specialty weekend came at the end of July. The day before the Specialty at Ventura, Ch. Briarwyn's Bright Star took the top honors in the breed. The Specialty itself, held with Santa Barbara, was judged by Harry Peters. The main winners were Ch. Madcap Syndicated News, BB for a second year and Jack Towne's Ch. Eyleland Double or Nothing, BOS.

The Eastern AWC Specialty moved to Delaware, Ohio in 1965. Judge Hollis Wilson gave BB to Silver Ho Kennels' Ch. Stoney Meadows Sharp Silver.

Dr. Sam Scott prepared a report on the year's show activities for the breed that appeared in the *Whippet News*. The breed was represented at 92%, or 473, of the 512 all-breed shows held during 1965. There were four BIS winners for the year. Ch. Greenbrae Barn Dance had two top awards and the imported Ch. Ringmore Finisterre had 11 GR1s.

Lots of interest and activity marked the year for the racing fraternity. The new Southern California Whippet Association's race meeting brought out a field of 28 adult starters. High point winner here was Ringo's Ringo, a dog who would be heard from a great deal. Second in earned points was Sing'n Little Girl Blue (Barlow).

The first race meeting of the Western Gazehound Club turned out very successfully. For Whippets, 18 adults were on hand with Urray Chieftain (Turpin, Sr.) the high point winner. It developed into a family affair this day with Rockabye Ember of Course, owned by William Turpin, Jr., getting high point puppy.

Ch. Greenbrae Barn Dance (Ch. Laguna Ligonier ex Ch. Greenbrae Laguna Lucia), owned by Mrs. Clare C. Hodge and bred by Alicia Yerburgh. Imported from England in the mid-1960s, this brindle and white became a multiple BIS winner and sired 56 champions up to this writing. *Gilbert.*

The official race meeting of the AWC, held at the Multanomah Greyhound track provided more than its share of excitement. Here Eyeland Hannah and Ringo's Ringo tied for high score. In the tie-breaking runoff, Hannah prevailed and was best in a good field of 37 adults. Hannah and Ringo also met at the race meeting held with the Santa Barbara Specialty amid much speculation and excitement on all sides. Here the results differed and Ringo's Ringo led the field and his arch rival. Top puppy honors went to Raindrop of Shamrock Lane (Stewart).

Again this year a large field was on hand for the races held with the International in Chicago. There were 59 adult starters with the first four finishers being Eyeland Hannah, Eyeland Homer, Ch. Rouget O'Lazeland and Bettebrook Bonita (Gutilla) respectively. The fastest time for the 475 foot course was 9.5 seconds.

Hurdle races at the same meeting drew a field of 15 with Moc's Lulubelle (Morgan) high point winner and Ch. Briarwyn's Bluestone (Martinez/Blackstone) second. High point puppy racer from a field of 20 was Rex (Varga).

Eyeland Park was the site of the Midwest Coursing Clubs' race meeting, an event which drew 43 adult starters. There was a tie here for high point winner involving Hasty Royal Red (Backman, Sr.) and Eyeland Hannah with third place to Grave Digger (Pegram). In the hurdle races Ch. Briarwyn's Bluestone led the field.

The magic number in the Midwest this year appeared to be 43 as the AWC race meeting in Marysville, Ohio drew the same number as the Eyeland Park meeting. Eyeland Homer was high point adult with Grave Digger finishing second. Renfield Bimmi (Renner) was high point winner among the 14 puppy starters.

The Mississippi Valley meeting also brought forward 43 dogs for the adult races. Eyeland Hannah notched another victory here, but it was a squeaker with Marial's War Paint (Strauss) second by a margin of two points. Renfield Anthony J. (Renner) was high point puppy and Moc's Lulubelle prevailed in the hurdle races.

The growth of Whippet racing is dependent on the enthusiastic efforts of its followers, and in 1965 Selwyn Blackstone and Gary Morgan staged exhibition races for Greyhounds and Whippets at the Sportsmens' show in Toronto. They also staged similar races at the Wisconsin State Fair in Milwaukee.

The *Whippet News* carried Louis Pegram's report showing that 14 dogs were rated Grade A racers in 1965, 34 were Grade B, 57 were Grade C and 70 were Grade D. Ringo's Ringo and Eyeland Hanna were the top racers of the year.

In England during 1965 the Whippet Club show drew 156 dogs with 276 entries. The BB was Greenbrae Poltesco Dusty Maid, just a year old at the time. Racing interest was also growing with the English fancy. There was organized coursing using live hares and the Whippet Coursing Club held its first meeting. The run for the Porthurst Cup was the featured event. Another new group, the Weldwyn Garden City Whippet Club was also started at this time. This Club planned events based on the weight categories of the racers. Seven separate divisions were planned. The major differences between British and American racing consisted of weight classes in Britain as against a grading system in the US and the practice of coursing live game in the UK compared to a mechanized lure in this country.

The fancy's attention was coming to rest more and more on Harlingen, Texas. From this base of operations Bettye Kirksey Scott's Dogpatch Kennels sent out the largest string of Whippets being shown in the United States at the time. The dogs were shown in the Southwest, Midwest and along the Pacific Coast by leading professional handlers and were definitely making their presence felt.

Also in 1965 the breed lost one of its staunchest supporters. Marjorie Hubbs Anderson died on July 12 thus closing the chapter on Mardomere. During its period of activity this kennel sent some of the finest into the ring, both imported and American-bred.

With the steady increase in all phases of breed activity, registrations took a big leap forward with 532 Whippets registered by the American Kennel Club in 1965.

1966

In view of sharply increased interest in the Whippet, it was decided that AWC activities in each of the three areas of the country, East, Midwest and Western, should be conducted by groups of area fanciers. This took in Specialties, supported shows and race meetings. The AWC Board worked closely with those in direct charge of the Club functions and the mutual cooperation made for a successful, satisfying year of Whippet progress.

The Whippet population was burgeoning and more puppies were available for sale now than at any time since the breed's introduction to the United States. Newer breeders soon realized that breeding a good dog to a good bitch, even with compatible pedigrees, did not guarantee puppies as good or better than the parents. It takes breeding many to come up with the exceptional few.

Show ring and race track competition at this time was very strong. Those who could, pursued heavy breeding programs to come up with the highest-quality campaigners. As a result a prospective buyer could often purchase just the puppy he wanted and at the right price.

Mrs. Philip Fell had the judging duties at the 1966 Westminster show.

She chose Dorothea Hastings' Ch. Eyleland Brown Betty for BB and Stoney Meadows Bold Venture for BOS. At the Midwest AWC Specialty, held in Chicago the day before International, Ch. Greenbrae Barn Dance, owned by Mrs. Clare Hodge, was BB under William Schmick in an entry of 62. Ch. Pennyworth Mother Goose was BOS. The next day Barn Dance repeated his Specialty win under Mrs. Augustus Riggs, IV who also made Pennyworth Nice Enough BOS this day.

The Western Specialty was again held with Santa Barbara with Mr. Schmick performing his second Specialty assignment for the year. His BB here was Jay Hyman's Ch. Highlight's Lucky Boy with BOS to Jeanette Keppleman's Ch. Madcap Stage Struck.

The beautiful Washington suburb of Gaitherburg, Maryland was the scene of the 1966 Eastern Specialty. Kay Finch wore the judge's badge this day and sent Ch. Morshor's Hop-to-it-Girl into the winners' circle as BB with her sire, Barn Dance the BOS in a field of 21 champions.

The year's show statistics revealed that Whippets were entered in 95% of the all-breed shows held in America. The year's top winners were Ch. Greenbrae Barn Dance (Hodge)—1 BIS, 10 GR1s, 7 GR2s, 10 GR3s, 1 GR4; Ch. Pennyworth Mother Goose (Newcombe)—1 BIS, 2 GR1s, 1 GR2; Bonnie of Blue Beaver (Green)—1 BIS, 1 GR1; Ch. Stoney Meadows Royal Fortune (Frailey)—6 GR1s, 6 GR2s, 8 GR3s, 4 GR4s.

As with show activities, the year's racing calendar was a full and exciting one. The International race meeting set a new record for the number of dogs entered, with 15 puppies, 14 for the hurdles and no less than 66 in the adult feature. High point honors in the puppy races went to Marial's Jelly Bean (Strauss), with the victory over the hurdles to Eyleland Handsome Ransom (Eyles). In the main event Eyleland Homer (Renner) came away with high point honors for the meeting.

A race meeting was held in conjunction with the Sun Maid Kennel Club of Fresno show with the Trounce family making a clean sweep in adult and puppy categories. Ringo's Ringo led the field of 18 adults while Bardon Sara Lawrence was high point puppy. It was the same story at the first match of the Northern California Whippet Fanciers, held this year. Sara Lawrence ran first among 11 puppies and Ringo did the same in a field of 18 adults. In conformation competition Madcap Time Limit, owned by Norman Ellis was Best Puppy in Match.

By this time the Midwest had become a strong center of Whippet racing activity and the 1966 racing season offered adequate proof of this. Following the record-breaking turnout at the International race meeting in early April, the Mississippi Valley meeting, held in mid-May, also set a new entry record. In a field of 50 adults Ch. Bettebrook Bonita (Hargis) tied with Eyleland Homer for high score. Following them across the finish line were Grave Digger and Heather Blue (Purvis) respectively. High point puppy was Traymatt Sumo (Steinberg). The meeting of the Midwest

Ch. Morshor's Whirlaway made a win record that lived up to his name. He became an American champion at eight months and had the Canadian title at 13 months. Retired early due to an accident, he left the ring a winner of six Groups and the top Whippet of 1967. In his retirement he sired over 60 champions. *Gilbert.*

Ch. Morshor's Hop-To-It-Girl, owned and handled by Frank T. Hill, was a litter sister to Whirlaway. She finished her championship at 10 months and is shown here being awarded BB at the 1966 AWC Eastern Specialty under judge Kay Finch. *Gilbert.*

Coursing Club in St. Charles, Illinois, drew 25 adult starters with high point honors going to Rex Ringo. He also turned the same trick at the Chain O' Lakes meeting in the same size field. Moc's Sam Junior won the hurdle races at the Midwest Coursing Club meet.

Whippet racing was featured at the Champaign, Illinois show as a special added attraction and 50 starters were on hand for the adult feature. Hasty Royal Red was the high point winner here with Whipoo's Whimson (Hopkins) high point puppy.

The Midwest Coursing Club held another meeting, this time in Antioch, Illinois, and had 46 starters for the adult race. It was another good day for Rex Ringo who notched another victory as high point winner. He was followed by Titan Hobo and Hasty Royal Red in that order. High point puppy was Caesar (Varga) with Renfield Shaun (Conrad) the winner in the hurdle race.

Another good turnout was on hand for the Marysville-Delaware, Ohio meeting. Forty-three adults were present here with the high point victory going to Eyleland Homer. Caesar was again high point puppy.

In addition to the meeting already reported there was regular activity at the home of William Backman, Sr. Whippet races were held on his farm during the summer months and the high point winners, based on total season average, were Hasty Royal Red and Fawn von Blaze. An added refinement for the Midwestern racing group was the introduction of a six-unit, collapsable starting box built by E. B. Hopkins. This was used at a number of the Midwestern race meetings and proved most satisfactory.

For the always-enthusiastic California contingent, racing was on the program at the West Coast AWC Specialty with Santa Barbara. The consistent speedster Ringo's Ringo was high point winner here with Urray Chieftain second.

The Pacific Northwest was the scene of Whippet racing excitement also in 1966. Racing was held along with the supported entry at the Olympic Kennel Club show (Washington). In a field of 34 starters Urray Chieftain nosed out Ch. Rockabye Ember of Course by one point! White Acres Sage (Babbit) ran third. Moving further north, the Western Gazehound Club conducted races at the University of British Columbia and drew 22 starters in adult races. Ember of Course was high point winner and also scored first in the runoff among the special program of races by weight categories.

The most significant racing development of 1966 was the announcement of the *Award of Racing Merit* program. This would commence on January 1, 1967 at all approved AWC race meetings. Another new development was the announcement of the first futurity to be held as part of the annual Marysville race meeting.

It was in 1966 that Mrs. Newcombe offered a new trophy for Best of Breed at the AWC Specialty show. This was a beautiful sterling silver piece that was offered to honor the memory of Donald Hostetter, owner of the Lazeland Whippets and a former AWC President. It was put into competition as a challenge trophy with three wins required for permanent possession.

The Whippet population kept up with activities and there were 618 American Kennel Club registrations for 1966.

1967

This year found the breed continuing in strong forward progress on various fronts. There was considerable activity in the show ring and among the growing number of racing enthusiasts. Whippets were a force to be reckoned with in every sense of the word.

The AWC Midwestern Specialty was held in Chicago with Mrs. Wear judging the breed. She chose Ch. Pennyworth Mother Goose for BB. The next day Harry Peters judged Whippets at International, selecting Mrs. Wear's Ch. Stoney Meadows Little Leonie to carry the Whippet colors into the Hound Group.

The always important, always well-attended Ventura/Santa Barbara weekend mustered large entries in 1967. Thelma Brown judging at Ventura found her BB winner in Mrs. Robert Henderson's Ch. Home Place Shandygaff while at Santa Barbara Marion Woodcock conferred top breed honors on Ch. Stoney Meadows Royal Fortune over an entry of 80.

The former handler Ellsworth Gamble judged the breed at Westminster and placed Ch. Greenbrae Barn Dance BB while at the Eastern Specialty Barney's daughter Ch. Morshor's Hop-To-It Girl won the same honor.

The AWC program of supporting shows was continuing with great success. The supported show in Renton, Washington was won by Ch. Hollypark Just Plain George, owned by Gladys Cutter. At Marysville, Ohio Alva Rosenberg gave BB to Ch. Pennyworth Mother Goose.

Canadian activity was much in evidence at this time. Kay Finch, judging the Western Gazehound Specialty, gave BB to Bardon's Faded Finery, owned by Doris Ringer. The Pacific National Exhibition (Vancouver, B.C.) put on three shows in the same location and three different dogs were BB winners here. They were Ch. Thane Jenny of Rose Dawn, Hobo Hills' Rambling Here and There and Ch. Urray Wild Bill, CD.

In England Ch. Laguna Ravensdown Astri was cutting a wide swath in the breed awards. She was BB at Crufts under Catherine Hodgson in 1967 and was a BIS winner with 13 C.C.'s on her record. She was owned by Mr. and Mrs. H. Wood. Mrs. Chapman's Moonlight and Roses was BIS at the Whippet Club championship show over 152 dogs in 246 entries and Pepper Preston got the nod for best at the same Club's open show over 134 dogs in 246 entries.

On the racing side of the picture the Mississippi Valley races brought out 37 adult starters. Strathoak Spring Intrigue (Pegram) was high point. Sir Winston of Woodlands (Whitworth) was high point puppy over 10 starters. At the Northern California Whippet Fanciers Association (NCWFA) official race meeting 25 starters were on hand. High point adult was Ringo's Ringo. At Champaign, Illinois Hasty Royal Red and Titan Hobo tied for high point honors in a field of 35 adult starters while the litter brothers Floating World and Final Word, owned by the author, finished 1st and 2nd in the puppy races. Strathoak Spring Intrigue and Bardon Sarah Lawrence were tied for high point honors at the International race meeting among 55 adults. Final Word and Floating World again were 1st and 2nd in the puppy races.

Special excitement marked the 1967 race meeting at Santa Barbara. Here Bardon Sarah Lawrence defeated the celebrated Ringo's Ringo. Ch. Bay Star Open Road (Turpin, Jr.) was high point winner at the Western Gazehound Club meeting in a field of 29 adult starters.

An interesting report by William Backman, Sr., writing in the *Whippet News*, disclosed that the total purse for the Marysville futurity amounted to $465.00. The first prize winner of this important event was Strathoak Spring Intrigue, owned by the author.

The Olympic Races had 25 adult starters with high point honors going to Ch. Sing'n Little Girl Blue (Barlow) while the Marysville National meeting had 52 with Ch. Rockabye Ember of Course the ultimate winner by only one point. Elsewhere in the Midwest, at the Eyleland Park National meeting, Caesar was the high point winner with a field of 53 adults. In the hurdle races Duke of Darling (Scroggins) was the winner.

Pinetops Opening Night (Hammond) was the top racer at the Antelope Valley meeting. There were 25 adult starters on hand for this affair.

The first dog to qualify for the Award of Racing Merit met all the qualifications during 1967. He was the author's Strathoak Spring Intrigue bred by Christine Cormany.

The year was marked by the passing of two prime movers in the ranks of Whippet fanciers. James Young died in November at the age of 85. He was one of the pioneers of the breed in the show ring and on the track. His daughter, Christine Cormany still carries on for the well-being of the breed. Arthur Mateikat, the impetus behind Whippet racing at the Carthage Fair in Cincinnati, Ohio, died in late December.

Whippet registrations experienced a slight rise in 1967 from the previous year. The American Kennel Club registered 655 of the breed while 1,732 were registered with the Kennel Club (England).

Ch. Pennyworth Mother Goose (left) by Ch. Courtenay Fleetfoot of Pennyworth out of Ch. Legend O'Lazeland, owned, bred and handled by Margaret P.
Newcombe, is pictured winning one of her three AWC Specialty bests to retire
the Donald Hostetter Memorial Trophy under A Peter Knoop. Ch. Greenbrae
Barn Dance was BOS, handled by Dorothy Hardy. *Gilbert.*

The Stud Dog class at the 1967 Eastern AWC Specialty was won by Ch. Stoney
Meadows Bold Chance (center), handled by Mrs. W. Potter Wear. Shown with
him are his son Ch. Stoney Meadows Double JC, handled by Damara Bolte,
who was also WD and his daughter Ch. Stoney Meadows Sealark, handled by
Anne Rogers Clark, who was BW. *Gilbert.*

Ch. Rolling's Lithe Tempest, owned by D.
Jay Hyman, was one of the foundations of
the Rolling Whippets. She is shown handled by her owner while his young son
looks on.   *Gilbert*.

Ch. Highlight's Lucky
Boy, owned and han-
dled by D. Jay Hyman,
was a strong and con-
sistent winner during
the 1960s. His wins in-
clude the AWC Western
Specialty at Santa Bar-
bara.   *Ludwig*.

This year started in high gear early. Mrs. W. Potter Wear had the task of sorting out the entries at Westminster. Her choice for BB came from the open bitch class in Calvin Perry's Pennyworth Merrie Xmas. A Westminster BB is always a good win, but when it is scored by a class entry over the top champions in the breed from every part of the country it does stand as something extra special.

There was a Whippet brace entered at Westminster in 1968. The dogs that composed it were owned by Anne and James Clark. As they were the only brace entered in breed they automatically competed in the Group. But from here they went on to capture Group first and then swept to BEST BRACE IN SHOW under the late Major B. Godsol. Jim Clark handled this beautifully matched pair to the first such win for the breed in history. The last night of the old Garden was a night to remember for everyone in the Whippet fancy.

The Midwest AWC Specialty was held again on the eve of the International show in early April. Sixty Whippets turned out to receive the opinion of Margaret Newcombe this day. Her BB was Ch. Highlight's Cleopatra, owned by Mrs. Clare Hodge with BOS going to Ch. Seyberne Gallant Fox owned by Morshor Kennels. The next day at International Mrs. Hodge scored a good double! Here, under judge Ellsworth Gamble, Cleopatra repeated her BB win of the day before and her father, Ch. Greenbrae Barn Dance was BOS. It is of interest to note that Barn Dance was BB at Westminster 14 months earlier under the same judge Gamble.

The California Specialty weekend began with an entry of 56 at Ventura. The BB was Ch. Stoney Meadows Royal Fortune who advanced to win the Hound Group. The next day the AWC Western Specialty was held, again with the Santa Barbara show. Mrs. Philip Fell judged the 69 dogs present and awarded the BB to Mrs. Robert Henderson's Ch. Home Place Shandygaff.

The Rock Creek show played host to the 1968 Eastern AWC Specialty. Here the eminent Percy Roberts passed on a fine entry of 72 Whippets. Mrs. Newcombe's Ch. Pennyworth Mother Goose was BB, retiring the Donald Hostetter Trophy. Ch. Gortico Flicker, owned by Mr. and Mrs. Joseph Pinkosz was selected BOS.

The Specialty of the Western Gazehound Club in Canada had an entry of 42 dogs. Ch. Rockabye Tolly, owned by Pamela Arthur, was BB and Ch. Stars and Stripes of Suntan, owned by R. Webster was BOS.

In addition to these Specialties many other shows had large Whippet entries with quality competition. That good dogs were being shown in many areas is proven by the numbers of good intervariety wins scored by Whippets during 1968.

The Award of Racing Merit program was now a special incentive for

Ch. Kirklea Court of Love with his owner Cora
Miller. *Tassone.*

Ch. Stoney Meadows Royal Fortune,
owned by Joan and H. G. Frailey, was one
of the most memorable dogs campaigned
on the West Coast. "Gridley" was a Specialty, Group and multiple BIS winner.
Furstner.

those who were interested in racing their dogs. Whippets that could go from the track to the ring with equal success were by no means unusual. This desirable situation was helped by the numerous programs put on by various groups to promote the Whippet that could show and race.

Bardon Sarah Lawrence was the high point winner at the Fresno meeting over 30 adult starters. The International meeting, with its full program, drew 56 adult starters, 18 puppies and 15 for the hurdle races. High point adult winner was Titan Hobo with Remney's Harlequin Vic (Backman, Jr.) leading the field in puppies and Duke of Darling prevailing in the hurdle races.

Titan Hobo and Harlequin Vic repeated their Chicago performances at the Mississippi Valley meeting with Eyleland Hurry Up Harry (Eyles) the winner over the hurdles. There were 49 adult starters on hand here. Titan Hobo also won the Champaign, Illinois meeting over a field of 43.

Pinetop's Opening Knight (Hammond-Ellis) was making his presence felt on the track and in the ring during 1968. He was high point race winner at the NCWFA meeting while at the Santa Barbara meeting with 39 adult starters, he ran a razor-close race with Ch. Sing'n Little Girl Blue. The latter prevailed by one point, but the race was close enough to bring about an adjustment in the point system in the official rules.

Other significant race results during 1968 include the Carthage Fair meeting where Ch. Marial's Jellybean and Strathoak Spring Intrigue tied for high points in a field of 36. Paul Fraser's Rockabye Emberson of Course won several important races in 1968. Western Gazehound Club meeting, Tacoma meeting and Marysville, Ohio all were won by this dog. At Marysville there were 58 starters in the adult races. There were also 15 puppies on hand with the winner here being Renfield Lady O'Lazebrook (Gutilla).

Whippet Races were featured at the Van Wert County (Ohio) fair with Eyleland Homer the winner in a field of 26 entries. The Eyleland Park National meeting had 50 adult starters and was a clean sweep for Louis Pegram. Strathoak Spring Intrigue was high point adult and Sweep It Clean and Hey Mouse finished 1st and 2nd among the 14 puppies. Art Mateikat's Royal Robin was 1st in the limit class.

In English racing an effort was launched to get the 84 race clubs in the North to race only Kennel Club registered dogs. While 34 clubs participated in the program, many prefer their own race club registrations to Kennel Club registrations. The principal variance between American racing and its British counterpart continued to be the British grading their racers by weight and the Americans basing classification on performance.

In 1968 Bardon Sarah Lawrence, owned by Lynn Trounce earned the AWC Award of Racing Merit.

There was a new editor for the *Whippet News* in the person of Christine Cormany with Joan Frailey and Don Dye serving as associate editors.

Under these people the *Whippet News* featured numerous useful articles on a wide variety of interesting subjects written by many of the most respected names in the breed.

A survey was conducted by the AWC of its membership and President Victor Renner, writing in the AWC organ, reported unanimous support for the concept of a single Standard, approximately 70% of the membership were in favor of racing, and 17% were opposed. On the question of what to breed for, 7½% were in favor of breeding for conformation only while 3% opposed breeding for racing and conformation. On other questions, 22% indicated they did not race their show dogs and 10% felt that show ring disqualifications should not bar a Whippet from competing on the track.

Whippet registrations surged in 1968 with 806 American Kennel Club registrations and 1,805 registrations processed by the Kennel Club (England).

1969

Times were rapidly changing and with them the styles of dog keeping. AWC President Victor Renner reported to Club members that for many years the Parent Club was kept afloat by a handful of dedicated breeders who, in most cases, kept large numbers of dogs. In 1969 the membership of the AWC had increased to 160 and was still growing. While the typical Club member in 1969 was just as devoted to the Whippet as his earlier counterparts, he kept far fewer dogs. Most looked upon Whippets as a family hobby with the dog or dogs acting as the family pet between shows or racing outings. It was the President's prediction that the trend would continue, and so it has. Interest in the Whippet has increased in the Pacific Northwest and over into Western Canada, while support was strong for the three parent Specialties and nine supported shows held during 1969.

Ch. Pennyworth Merrie Xmas made it two Westminsters in a row by winning BB at the 1969 installment under W. W. Brainard, Jr. Ch. Stoney Meadows Royal Fortune was on hand from California and was awarded BOS.

It is of interest to note that Royal Fortune, whose call name was "Gridley," boasted a most impressive show record. In 1969 he had five BIS, 21 GR1s, 1 Specialty BB and 100 BBs at all-breed shows. He was handled by E. R. Hastings for owners Mr. and Mrs. H. G. Frailey.

Another Whippet that was making its presence felt was the great bitch Ch. Winterfold Bold Bid who was acquired by Morshor Kennels from Martine Collings the previous year. At this point her record included five BIS, and 18 GR1s.

Ch. Stoney Meadows Imp of Satan, owned by Dianne T. Horton became a champion at one year and produced 14 champions from Ch. Morshor's Whirlaway and Ch. Pennyworth Would You Believe. *Gilbert.*

Ch.Morshor's Minuet, a Group-winning litter sister to Whirlaway and Hop-To-It-Girl, finshed when she was 11 months old. *Gilbert.*

Ch. Pennyworth Merrie Xmas, owned by Barbara Collins was an outstanding winner as well as a top producer. She was BB at Westminster in 1968 and 1969 and was a Group winner.

A classic study of Whippets in action—Ch. Madcap Dusty Road (#2) and Ch. Sing'n

Little Girl Blue (#4) show their determination and intensity in a run for the lure.

Comer

Several dogs came to the fore for their ability to sire quality. Ch. Courtenay Fleetfoot of Pennyworth had, at this point, 41 champion get. He had already been named top producing Hound for 1965 and tied for top producer of all breeds in 1966. Ch. Morshor's Whirlaway at four years had already sired 14 champions.

Obedience was drawing considerable interest at the end of the 1960s. Articles on the subject continue to appear in the *Whippet News* with its supporters advocating more Whippets in training. A Whippet had not annexed the CDX degree in four years prior to 1969. Then Baronhoff's Hustler won the degree followed soon by Spiral Swing and Sway. A strong obedience booster was 13-year-old Linda Blalock who was training several Whippets to their CD degrees. Ch. Forest Slim Jim qualified for the CD with a score of 194½ at the age of eight years. Another noteworthy obedience Whippet Ch. Rocket's Torpedo, CDX was the sire of Shylo Agile Artemis who also had the CDX degree. This too can run in families.

The AWC program of supported entries at shows in various sections of the country was proving itself with every passing year. Examples of successful supported affairs that were held in 1969 included the Delaware Ohio show where Ch. Coventry's Jumping Jupiter, owned by Pennyworth Kennels was BB in an entry of 26. In the Pacific Northwest, a supported entry was held with the Tacoma, Washington show where the BB winner was Doris Ringer's Bardon's Faded Finery. Canada also conducts supported shows, but calls them boosters. At the Western Gazehound booster in British Columbia Ch. Stars and Stripes of Suntan was BB in 1969. This dog was owned by Mr. and Mrs. R. M. Webster.

During the previous year Mary Beth Arthur mailed a survey to licensed Whippet judges and the results became available in 1969. Of the many points made by those who answered the various questions, most decried the awarding of show ring honors to dogs that display the undesirable "hackney-gait."

The year 1969 was another fruitful one for the Whippet on the race track. The California racer Pinetop's Opening Knight has now become a champion and scored a host of impressive track victories in the current season. These included Antelope Valley over 39 adult starters, Southern California Whippet Association over 20 starters, Santa Barbara with 36 starters and Sir Frances Drake KC races in a field of 21 starters.

Whirlaway Magnificent Lance (Grimm) was the high point winner at the NCWFA meet. Thirty starters turned out for this meeting.

In the Pacific Northwest Emberson of Course was enjoying a good season and won the Western Gazehound meeting over 20 starters and the Northwest Whippet Fanciers' Meeting over 23.

The Mississippi Valley meeting offered a full program and put on a very well-attended affair. Renfield Lady O'Lazebrook was high point adult in a field of 43 while Riverdale's Charmaine (Purvis) led 17 others in the puppy races. Nine starters were on hand for the hurdle races and the winner was Dreyfus Dardonus (Robbins).

Another large turnout was the order of the day at Champaign, Illinois. Here Fortuna Fair Annet (Robinson) prevailed over her 46 rivals while Brenda's Brandy (Clift) was high point among 18 puppies.

At the Marysville, Ohio meeting a large field of 53 adults were on hand. Renfield Lady O'Lazebrook, tied for top honors with Scram Whisper (Klintworth-Blackstone). The Marysville Futurity involved a total purse of $540.00 split between 21 high point winners at the 1969 meeting.

In other Midwest events a field of 46 raced at the Carthage Fair meeting. It was a tie for high point honors between Brenda's Champagne (Clift) and Fortuna Fair Annet. It was another victory for Caesar at the 1969 Eyleland Park meeting. His triumph over 42 others brought the Raczak trophy home to owner Gaza Varga. It was also announced this year that the Midwest Coursing Club would conduct a puppy race futurity at Eyleland Park.

Four dogs earned their Award of Racing Merit (ARM) certificate in 1969. They were Caesar, Emberson of Course, Ch. Rockabye Ember of Course and Ch. Marial's Jelly Bean, CD. Jelly Bean was the first Whippet to become titled in conformation and obedience to hold the ARM.

In 1969 there was a very slight decline in registrations with the American Kennel Club while the Kennel Club (England) registered more than in 1968. The numbers were 797 and 2,025 respectively.

1970

The matter of size was on the minds of many Whippet fanciers as the decade of the seventies began. Gradually the dogs seen coming to the top in the show ring and on the track were larger than their predecessors. And this was as true for bitches as for dogs. Whippets measuring in excess of 23 inches at the shoulder were causing both controversy and concern.

Support for the larger dogs came primarily from those who favored the so-called American type and from race enthusiasts who found that the larger dog's chances at the track were better than those of his smaller rivals. This support constituted about 25% of the voting membership of the AWC.

It was at this time that the author was serving as AWC Racing Secretary. In this post he received a written vote by a majority of the Board and the Sectional Racing Rules Committee to limit the size of racing dogs. The ruling limited the size of dogs to no more than 24 inches at the shoulder and/or above 40 pounds. Bitches could not exceed 23 inches at the shoulder and could weigh no more than 35 pounds.

Backers of the larger dogs vigorously opposed the Board and did what

David Rosenstock starting a field of Whippets at Santa Barbara races held with the Western AWC Specialty. The attention of each dog is firmly riveted on the lure. In the top picture on the facing page Ch. Pinetop's Opening Knight (center) starts to make his move to victory and in the bottom photo the field surges to the finish line. The tremendous effort these dogs expend in racing is obvious in this dramatically exciting study.

they could to maintain the integrity of the animals they favored. However, the Board moved toward making changes in the Standard. These changes were concerned with size, general appearance and several other points such as eyes and teeth.

Any change in a breed Standard involves a considerable amount of time. The suggested changes must be submitted to the AKC by the Parent Club of the breed concerned. If AKC has no objections to the proposed changes, they (the changes) are submitted to a vote of the breed club membership. If the majority of the membership casts ballots in favor of the proposed new Standard, it (the Standard) is then published on the Secretary's page of *Pure-Bred Dogs—American Kennel Gazette* for two months. This allows anyone who wishes, the time to write the AKC Board of Directors, pro or con. The proposed new Standard then goes back to the Board for approval, rejection or further alteration. This is a process that can take up to two years in some cases.

Mrs. Philip Fell, just returned from a 10-year sojourn in England, judged Whippets at the 1970 Westminster show. In an entry of 47 and with a top-quality collection of champions, she chose the well-known California winner Ch. Home Place Shandygaff owned by Mrs. Robert Henderson and James McManus for BB. Mrs. Wear judged the AWC Specialty at Nashville, Tennessee, a growing area of Whippet interest. From the entry of 36 Ch. Morshor's Happy Forecast came away with BB for owner Booth E. Roberts.

At the AWC Specialty weekend in California Ventura's BB winner was Ch. Hollypark Good Lord Chumley while at the Specialty, again with Santa Barbara, Frederica Page's Ch. Humble Acres Happy Chance won the nod for BB in the 109-entry field. Ch. Cinnabar Kiwi of Flying W, owned by Bob and Alice Dildine, was BOS. The Specialty was judged by Eugene Jacobs.

In the East the Parent Specialty was held with the Boardwalk KC show in Atlantic City, New Jersey. Here Christine Cormany drew the impressive entry of 126 dogs. Her BB was Ch. Sie Wals Navigator, owned by L. C. and Ellis Klimpel. Morshor's Martini on the Rocks, owned by Pennyworth Kennels, was BOS and Bwa' Rangis Dan Patches, owned by M. Payne and Barbara Briggs was BW.

On the racing scene several up-and-coming dogs from the previous year were having good seasons on the track in 1970. These included Ch. Pinetops' Opening Knight who was high point winner at Pomona and Whirlaways Magnificent Lance, high point at NCWFA meeting over 25 adult starters. Lance also ran a dead heat for first with Babuska of Hillcrest at the SCWA meeting.

The Klintworth-Blackstone combination was really making heads turn with the determined speedster Scram Whisper. In 1970 this dog was the high point winner at the race meetings of the International show with 52

114

The top race Whippet of 1968 was Titan Hobo. Here AWC President Victor Renner presents the trophy for Hobo's achievements to his owner Henry Raczak while the Raczak children share the moment. The presentation was made during the Mississippi Valley KC show.

Whippets are for showing and Whippets are for racing, but Whippets are also for loving. Mr. and Mrs. Charles Billings, relaxing with a group of their "Flyalongs," are typical of most Whippet owners who know and appreciate the breed's value as a companion.

adults, Santa Barbara over 54, Mississippi Valley with 50 and Champaign with 56. Scram I'm First (Blackstone-Fisher), a litter brother to Whisper, managed to live up to his name at Antioch and Marysville in fields of 46 and 51 respectively.

Emberson of Course was now a champion and was still burning up the tracks in the Pacific Northwest. He was high point adult at the British Columbia Racing Club meeting in a field of 27 and at Tacoma in a field of 21 adult starters.

International also had 19 puppies at its meeting. High points for first were divided between Billmar Blaze and Billmar Blitz (Tetzlaff). In the puppy races at Santa Barbara Epinard's Sonny Jim of Course (Fraser) was high point in a field of 12 starters while Rolsan Gingerbread Boy (Kinch) prevailed in the puppy field of 21 at Mississippi Valley. At the British Columbia Club meeting the high point puppy was Sunny Side Up of Course (Lyttle) in a field of 12.

The 1970 Carthage Fair meeting drew 53 adult starters with high point going to Riverdale's Charmaine (Purvis) and the puppy races yielding another high point win to Sunny Side Up of Course. Epinard's Sonny Jim of Course was also the winner among the puppies at Tacoma. The puppy contest at the Champaign, Illinois meeting resulted in a tie score for Fool's Gold (Emerich) and Titan Sassy Miss (Niehoff). There were 11 puppies on hand for this meeting.

Fortuna Fair Annet found the day to suit her at the Hamilton, Ohio meeting. Here she was high point over a large field of 46 adult starters.

The *Whippet News* continued to provide a wide spectrum of useful information to members of the AWC. One article of particular interest came from Ernest Rickard dealing with sighthound racing in Continental Europe. In the Germanic languages a sighthound is called a *windhund* and the article also noted that Whippets are the most popular breed in the sport there. Also bitches outnumber dogs on the track by almost four to one.

Another *Whippet News* article, this by Dr. Robert Pruett, offered an interesting percentage breakdown of Whippet entries at American shows. The article revealed that the average entry at an all-breed show was 11.06: 3.69 dogs; 4.84 bitches; 2.53 champions. There were major entries for dogs in 25% of the 550 shows reviewed for this survey and majors for bitches in 30% of these same shows. It is of interest to note that AKC uses, as a rule of thumb, a 20% figure for the number of major shows for a breed against the total of all shows. As competition grows in any given section of the country, AKC will determine whether to adjust the point rating so that majors are not too easy to find, which is as it should be.

A veteran fancier passed away in August of 1970. This was Miss Judith R. Shearer of the Meander Whippets.

Registrations were steadily climbing with 928 dogs added to the rolls of

As much at home on 200 acres of green as 200 yards of track—These are a group of Mr. and Mrs. Philip S. P. Fell's Badgwood Whippets with their owners. This stately painting, by Jean Bowman, was executed in 1967 while the Fells lived in Kent, England. The Whippets shown are (from left) Badgewood Copper Penny, Ch. Michael of Meander, Badgewood Charlottesvlle and Eng. Ch. Badgwood Sewickley. Also shown in this grouping are three of the Fells' Norwich Terriers, a breed they have made long-term, strong successes in.

the American Kennel Club and 2,038 registered with the Kennel Club (England).

1971

Firm proof of the growing interest in Whippets came to light by the formation of several new groups of fanciers that have been organized in various parts of the country. The Atlantic Whippet Association was formed in the Northeast while in Southern California the Great Western Whippet Club was getting active with plans for exhibition racing as part of the Silver Bay KC of San Diego all-breed show. Plans were also underway for a group to be known as the Mid-America Whippet Fanciers.

Westminster had 48 dogs in competition this year with good majors in both sexes. Judge Mrs. A. V. Riggs, IV gave David Harmon's Ch. Morshor's Airborne BB and the Millers' Ch. Morshor's Mischievous Imp BOS.

The AWC supported a number of important shows according to its policy to encourage good entries. At International Mrs. Fell placed Ch. Morshor's Martini On the Rocks, owned by Pennyworth Kennels, BB in an entry of 36.

The AWC also supported the Bryn Mawr and Tuxedo Park entries. At the former Mrs. Newcombe drew 39 entries and awarded BB to Mrs. Clare Hodge's Ch. Highlight's Dragnetta while at Tuxedo Dr. William Houpt found his best one in the W. Potter Wears' Ch. Stoney Meadows Volare as the best of a field of 54.

Mrs. C. Wescott Gallup judged 114 Whippets at the Western AWC Specialty selecting Mrs. Henry Speight's Pathen's Sasha of Carrob for BB. The East Coast Specialty, held with the Boardwalk KC, brought out 66 dogs for judge Leonard Gilman. It was a good day for dogs carrying the Morshor prefix, as BB was awarded to Ch. Morshor's Happy Forecast and BOS went to Ch. Morshor's Martini on the Rocks, owned by Pennyworth Kennels.

From Canada came the good news that Strip Tease of Course (Stacey-Cucheran) was BB at the Western Gazehound Club show in an entry of 36 and went on to bring BIS honors home.

Just as interest and activity made steady gains in the show ring in 1971, racing with Whippets was a growing pastime. The AWC passed the control of approved race meetings to groups of fanciers in local areas around the country. In view of the tremendous growth of the sport this must be considered both practical and prudent.

It was encouraging that many of the good race dogs of the past two seasons were still doing well on the track and that many young speedsters were showing good promise of things to come. One such was Ch. Pine-

Badgewood Belle Starr, owned, bred and handled by Mrs. Fell was first in Veterans under Mrs. Cormany at the 1970 AWC Eastern Specialty. *Gilbert.*

Ch. Morshor's Martini On the Rocks, owned and handled by Margaret P. Newcombe is shown scoring BB at International 1971 under Mrs. Fell. *Ritter.*

top's Opening Knight who took high point honors at the Fresno meeting in a field of 38 adult starters. R.S.K. Jude (Kubat) was high point puppy here. Opening Knight also had victories at the SCWA over 33 rivals and at Santa Barbara over 54.

Scram I'm First, who had some good runs in 1970, continued as a strong threat in Midwestern race meetings. His victories include the Eyleland Park and Hamilton, Ohio meetings with 54 and 42 adult starters, respectively. At both these affairs the high point puppy was a youngster with the unlikely name of Volant's Fat Albert (Helton).

The International meeting, by now an institution, brought together a field of 61 adult starters. Brenda's Brandy was high point adult, Brother Abraham (Kennedy) was high point puppy in a field of 13 and a tie occurred for first in the hurdle races between Eyleland Harry and Shadow Boxer, both owned by Ralph Eyles.

The NCWFA meeting in San Jose drew a field of 26 adults with the high point honors going to Whirlaway Apache (Hayhurst). The same group held a race meeting at Salinas and here Heathcliffe Basha (Yasunaga) tied for high point honors with Epinard's Shelby of Wyndsor (Balint) with 31 adult starters. The NCWFA meeting at Santa Clara with 27 starters had the same two dogs tied for high point honors. This group also held a field coursing trial. The winner among 36 was Coventry Sailor of Regalstock (Rosenstock).

A young California contestant also worthy of notice in this year was Whirlaway's Tera of Ortman Farms. This dog was the winner of high point puppy honors at Santa Barbara and Salinas.

In the Pacific Northwest Epinard's Sonny Jim of Course was high point adult at the British Columbia meeting in a field of 29 while Renfield Temptress of Course was the puppy winner.

The Carthage Fair meeting drew a large field of 58 and the winner was the author's Change in Destiny. Eighteen puppies were also on hand here and the winner in this department was Destructor (Tolley).

An important decision by the AWC Board, made during the Eastern Specialty, concerned the breed Standard and racing dogs. It was decided that disqualifications in the Standard should also apply to dogs participating in all AWC approved ARM meetings.

With 241 people on the rolls, the American Whippet Club's membership stood at an all time high. The President, Victor Renner emphasized the need to develop members toward being able to assume positions of responsibility within the Club. It was felt this would insure the continuity of Whippet activities being conducted by the Parent Club in the future as they had been up to this point.

American registrations experienced a very slight drop in 1971 to 923, but English registrations were sharply down with 1,726.

Ch. Stoney Meadows Volare (Ch. Morshor's Whirlaway ex Stoney Meadows Hell's Angel), owned, bred and handled by Mrs. W. P. Wear was BW at Westminster 1971 under Mrs. Augustus V. Riggs, IV, enroute to his title.

Shafer.

Ch. Badgewood Dixie, owned, bred and handled by Mrs. Fell, was BW at Hatboro (Pennsylvania) under Mrs. M. Lynwood Walton enroute to her championship.

Gilbert.

Ch. Badgewood The Plainsman, owned, bred and handled by Mrs. Fell. *Klein*.

Ch. Stoney Meadows Magnific (Stoney Meadows Royal Venture ex Ch. Stoney Meadows Fairy Fox), owned and bred by the Potter Wears, has shown himself a strong producer of race Whippets as well as show dogs. *Gilbert*.

Ch. Stoney Meadows Royal Flight (Ch. Stoney Meadows Volare ex Stoney Meadows Bold Queen), owned and bred by Mr. and Mrs. W. Potter Wear. *Klein*.

In an open letter to members of the AWC, President Victor Renner stressed the need for better communication among Club members and also the need for delegating the responsibilities of the Club's affairs. He reminded Club members that the primary functions of the AWC were the *Whippet News*, the maintenance of the Standard and the establishment of policy, program and Club awards that will be of benefit to the majority of the membership. He also sounded a warning against the selection of people for key posts in the Club that were not assertive enough or that sought position in the Club to enhance their own place in the dog game.

In an important decision the AWC Board requested the National Racing Secretary to revise the official rules so that monorchids and cryptorchids would be barred from official racing. The AWC would also take no part in racing where monetary wagering was permitted.

In 1972 Victor Renner asked to be relieved of the AWC Presidency. Mrs. Philip S. P. Fell came into the office, and in so doing, became the second woman President of the AWC in its 42 year history. Mrs. Fell has been a member of the AWC since 1939. Upon his resignation from the presidency Victor Renner became the AWC Delegate to the AKC.

The Parent Club began to issue its own Certificates of Accomplishment to member-owned dogs. These were given for junior showmanship, new champions and obedience degrees.

Still another new group was formed at this time. It was the Tri-State Whippet Club and had its area of operations in Ohio. Gary Purvis and Dona Helton served as first President and Secretary respectively.

At Westminster this year Whippets came under the scrutiny of the eminent British authority Judy De Casembroot. From an entry of 43 Ch. Morshor's Flamboyant, owned by T. A. De Sousa and Gail Volavka, emerged as BB. Ch. Stoney Meadows Moon Mist, owned by Mrs. Clare Hodge, was BOS. The entire Whippet fancy was treated to a bonus at Westminster in the junior showmanship win by Debbie Butt. The junior showmanship competition at Westminster brings the most talented young handlers in America together, and to win here is indeed a tremendous accomplishment.

International had a good turnout of 40 Whippets for judge Len Carey. Ch. Dress Circle Aces High was the eventual BB winner. He is owned by Mr. and Mrs. James Butt. Ch. Winterfold Image, owned by Isabel Chamberlain was chosen for BOS.

The AWC Specialties held during 1972 all had very large entries. The Midwest affair was the largest with 108, followed by Santa Barbara with 104 and finally the Eastern region had 74 dogs. Interestingly all three Specialties held this year took place within approximately seven weeks of each other.

The first was held on the West Coast. Ventura, the day before the Specialty, brought out 54 dogs for judge Tom G. Rainey. Ch. Pathens Sasha of Carrob was BB with Ch. Timbar's Artful Dodger BOS. Frederica Page judged the Specialty and made it two in a row for Sasha who went on to win a strong Hound Group under judge Ramona Jones. The well-known campaigner Ch. Stoney Meadows Royal Fortune was awarded BOS. This Specialty offered a Sweepstakes which was won by Pathens Shaitan of Carrob, owned by Pat Speight and Robert Whitmire. The judge was Hobart Stephenson.

Next came Ravenna which was the scene of the Midwest Specialty. Norman Ellis made Ch. Winterfold Bold Bid, owned by Diane T. Horton, his BB. The Specialty winner went from here to capture a quality Hound Group under judge A. Peter Knoop. Ch. Whipoo's Chances Are, owned by J. Ellis and R. M. Duncan was BOS. In Sweepstakes Marial's Renfield Phoebe, owned by Strauss-Arthur was the winner under the author.

Finally the Eastern Specialty took place as part of the Westchester show. Mrs. Wear judged the entry adding another jewel to the crown of Ch. Winterfold's Bold Bid by making her BB. The BOS came out of the puppy dog class. It was Ann Wanson's Westgate's Charley H.

Across the land many important shows were designated AWC supported. As a result competition at them was good and entries came from far and wide. At Champaign, Illinois Mrs. Wear gave Tony Maiullo's He Ain't Country the breed in an entry of 37. At Nashville Anne Clark judged and found her top Whippet in Louis and Sene Auslander's Ch. Alpine Ski Bum. There was an entry of 26 on hand.

Beverly Hills brought out 33 with AWC support. Alva Roseberg was the judge and sent Ch. Pathen's Sasha of Carrob into the Hound Group. The Santa Clara show was also supported and had a good entry of 60. The BB here was Ch. Home Place Barn Owl. The supported entry at the Sun Maid Kennel Club totaled 88 and the top spot went to Bud and Betty Carlson's Ch. Golden Rainbow.

The Tuxedo Park show which is held on the same weekend with Westchester was a supported show in the East. Like Santa Clara, this show had an entry of 60 for judge Kay Finch. Best of Breed was Larry Shaw's and C. N. Miller's Ch. Kirklea Flying Machine.

Several of the breed accounted for BIS wins during 1972. Ch. Amigo Amistaso Payso, C.D., owned by Nubby Haper (breeder) and Bruce Clark went to the top over 1800 dogs at the Colorado KC and Ch. Pathens Sasha of Carrob was BIS at Yellowstone Valley under Tom Stevenson.

On the racing scene a number of good speedsters came consistently to the fore thereby establishing their great ability on the track. The International race meeting had 51 adult starters in 1972. Brenda's Brandy took the high point honors here with Titan Cinnamon Tost (Weaver) the high point puppy.

Ch. Winterfold's Bold Bid (Ch. Coveydown Greenbrae Wayfarer ex Stoney Meadows Bold Queen), owned by Mr. and Mrs. James E. Butt and bred by Col. and Mrs. John Collins, is an all-time great of the breed. Her show record includes 10 BIS, 70 GR1s, 77 other placements and over 200 BBs. Her extended campaign went on long after lesser dogs have been retired from competition and includes a BIS in 1976. *Gilbert.*

The new Tri-State Club held a race meeting that drew 34 starters with the high point score made by Destructor. Among 10 puppies high points were won by Titan Cinnamon Tost. The Champaign meeting had a field of 55 adult starters on hand and the winner was Riverdale Royal Charmaine (Purvis). Antonio's Quick Silver (Maiullo) was high point puppy in a field of 18.

The Greater St. Louis Spring meeting drew 40 for the adult races with the win carried off by He Ain't Country while the puppy races resulted in another victory for Titan Cinnamon Tost.

He Ain't Country also had a good win at the Burlington, Iowa meeting, where he came out on top of a field of 23. At Carthage Fair meeting Riverdale Royal Charmaine led the field of 32 adults to capture high points, while at the St. Louis group's Fall meeting Destructor was the winner over a field of 38 adults.

On the West Coast Jean and Vince Balint's Epinard's Shelby of Wyndsor was having a banner year. This dog swept six race meetings and was named Top Racer of the Year.

Ch. Whirlaway's Apache made history by being the first Whippet with four titles: his championship, CD degree, ARM and Pacific Coursing Championship. Another memorable runner, Ch. Pinetop's Opening Knight, ARM, was doing great things as a sire. By 1972 he had fathered 14 champions and was considered one of the top sires of racing Whippets in the United States.

This was a year which also took its sad toll of important fanciers. Sibyl Jacobs died of cancer in April. With her husband, Eugene, she operated the Whipoo Kennels and bred many dogs that were successful both in the show ring and on the race track. Her active participation in the breed extended back almost 20 years. She had been an editor of the *Whippet News* and an officer and Board member of the Parent Club. The Jacobses had been responsible for developing a definite type in their breeding program and for assisting in the revival of Whippet racing by their activities with the International meeting. Mrs. E. B. Hopkins was another who passed away in 1972. She was active in obedience and was a member of the Champaign, Illinois KC. With her husband she co-owned the great racer Ch. Whipoo's Whimsy. Mrs. Hopkins was a fancier who enjoyed all the abilities of the Whippet breed.

The last of the Shearer sisters, Julia, died in 1972. With her sister she built a strong breeding establishment in the Meander Kennels. The Shearers began their kennels in 1930 and with the passing of Julia the Whippet fancy truly saw the end of an era.

Edging ever closer to the thousand mark in registrations, Whippets recorded 990 new individuals on the AKC's rolls in 1972 while the Kennel Club in England registered 2,003 dogs.

Ch. Sporting Fields Midnite Lace (Ch. Morshor's Bold N' Courageous ex Apprax-in Ebony O'Brien), owned and bred by Mr. and Mrs. James E. Butt and handled by daughter Jennifer, has had a good career in the breed ring and with her young owner in junior showmanship. The Sporting Fields Whippets are a true family affair.

Ashbey.

Ch. Dress Circle Aces High (Ch. Bettebrook Benchmark ex Ch. Dress Circle Royal Flush), owned by Mr. and Mrs. James E. Butt, was a top winner in the United States for 1972. Since retiring from the breed ring, he has been co-starring with Melissa Butt to carve a wide swath in junior showmanship competition.

Gilbert.

Ch. Charter Oak Me Did, owned and handled by Mrs. James E. Butt.   *Gilbert.*

The accent was on quality in 1973 with no shortage of good dogs competing in the show ring and on the race track. It is also worthy of note that no one individual dominated the action. This year would go on record as another good one in which the multi-faceted Whippet grew in importance in the entire dog world.

Margaret P. Campfield (formerly Newcombe) stood in the center of the ring at Westminster in 1973. From an entry of 36 Mrs. Campfield selected the BB winner from the Bred-by-Exhibitor bitch class. She was Hound-Hill Right As Rain, owned by Cora N. Miller and the BOS was a homebred of the Willard K. Denton's, Ch. Ardencaple's Magic Mist.

It was the steady campaigner Ch. Alpine Ski Bum who was BB in an entry of 37 at International under Anne Rogers Clark and later placed third in a hotly-contested Hound Group under A. Peter Knoop. The BOS came from the Open class in the form of Greyfriar's Flyalong Pippit, owned by Charles and Lillian Billings.

The AWC had its Western Specialty at San Rafael, California. Mrs. Campfield judged the 49 entries and awarded BB to Ch. Terrace Hill Jody of Roadway, owned by Joan Frailey and R. Housky and BOS to Pennyworth I'm A Believer, owned by B. M. Johnston and J. Slater.

The Midwest Specialty at Ravenna brought out a grand entry of 120 for judge Christine Cormany. Ch. Mare's Head Royal Blu Princess, bred and owned by JoAn Geise, rose to the top of this large collection while the BOS was Misty Moor's Royal Huntsman, owned by Audrey and Stephen Borrello, scoring spectacularly from the Junior Puppy Class! Best in Sweepstakes under Mrs. Wear was Heritage Kingpin, bred and owned by Dr. R. Schaubhut.

The Eastern Specialty was held at Westchester, two weeks after the Ravenna show, and marked another Specialty best for Royal Blu Princess. This time the judge was Anne Rogers Clark and 60 dogs were present. The BOS was Ch. Hound Hill Brattleboro, owned by Ben and Chris Pendick.

Like the Specialities, the supported shows had good entries and high fancier enthusiasm. The Old Dominion KC show, held in Reston, Virginia was a supported affair. It had an entry of 50 Whippets for Dr. M. Josephine Deubler who chose the BIS winning Ch. Winterfold's Bold Bid, now owned by Mr. and Mrs. James Butt as BB. On the same summer weekend with the Midwest Specialty the beautiful Chagrin Valley show drew a fine entry of 95 for Club President Betty Fell. The two main winners came from the classes at this show. The BB was Appraxin Leewayne Badfinger, owned by R. and P. Sapp while the BOS was Ramble Inn Acres Gibson Girl, owned by B. J. Lutz. On the East Coast an entry of 35 came together at Westbury for Thelma Brown. The great winner, Ch.

Ch. Fraserfield Waltz O'Starthaok with the veteran fancier Christine Cormany. *Schley.*

Ch. Mare's Head Royal Blu Princess (Mardomere Christmas Knight ex Gortico Amber Morn), owned and bred by JoAn Giese, boasts a record of two Specialty BBs, three supported entry BBs and five GR1s. She is shown in a strong BB under Heywood Hartley at Suffolk County, the owner handling. *Klein.*

129

Winterfold's Bold Bid took the breed here and followed by topping the Hound Group under Mrs. Wear and was BIS in a total entry of 1615 under William Brainard. This BIS was one of a number of top wins made by this fine bitch during the year. Handled by Robert Forsyth, Bold Bid was doing a good job for the breed by keeping the Whippet in the eye of Group and Best in Show judges. Westbury's BOS was Ch. Bon Mot Gordo, owned by Joan Bartlett.

Just as 1973 was a good year in the American show ring, it was noteworthy also in Canada. A new record was established by Canadian Ch. Night Talk of Woodsmoke in winning two BIS at only nine months old. At the Whippet Club of Canada, under Christine Cormany, Night Smoke, owned by Pat Waller, was BB and followed this with a GR1 and Best Canadian-Bred Hound.

Another dog that made a strong showing in 1973 was Ch. Dondelayo Buccaneer who had a BIS win at Nashville. And yet he had company in this year that top Whippets were so much in evidence. There was Ch. Pathens Sasha of Carrob, a winner of three BIS, two AWC Specialties and many BB. There was also Ch. Winterfold's Bold Bid, a top winner with the qualities of a laster. There was Mrs. Hodge's Ch. Stoney Meadows Moon Mist who, with four BIS and several other important wins, was establishing a record as one of the top Whippet bitches of all time. Ch. Mare's Head Royal Blu Princess a multiple Specialty winner stood out in this year and a new one came to the fancy's attention. This was the young bitch Ch. Runner's Our Own Charisma, owned by Isabell Stoffers from whom important things would soon be heard.

The racing scene was marked by continued successes of dogs that were strong on the track in previous seasons, and also by hard-charging newcomers that consistently set the pace and led the field in many of their races.

One of the holdovers was Destructor. Always a strong competitor at Midwestern race meetings, he was the high point winner at the International meeting over a field of 53 adult starters. The Northern California Whippet meeting at Fresno had a good turnout of 58 for the feature races. There was a tie for high point honors between Featherstone's Mr. Lightfoot (Steckel) and Renfield Temptress of Course (Rankin), Mr. Lightfoot had another important track victory in 1973 with the high point honors at the Great Western Whippet Association meeting. Held in Las Vegas, Nevada, the meeting attracted 32 dogs.

On the West Coast in 1973 a dog named Van Oorschoot's Toro, owned by Denna Marten, was making a place for himself in the permanent records of the breed. At the National Point Race meeting in Santa Barbara, Toro won all four of his races to emerge the best of a field of 61 adults. It was the same story at the Northwest Whippet Fanciers National meeting with Toro topping the four races he ran in. He went on to top the field of

41 at the NCWFA Santa Clara meeting, over 46 at the NCWC meeting in San Jose and at Great Western's second 1973 meeting he prevailed over a field of 42.

Van Oorschot's Toro surely proved himself on the Whippet track. He was a dog that kept excitement high in Whippet racing circles and was considered by many the best race Whippet in California since Ringo's Ringo made his great career in 1965.

Santa Barbara also offered racing for puppies at its meeting. Fourteen starters were on hand for the puppy races and the result was a dead heat for the high points. The co-winners were Crick-E Su's Spot (Valenti-Sawyer) and Topper's Wistful of Regalstock (Rosenstock).

In 1973 the South had it first AWC-approved race meeting. Twenty dogs took part in the qualifying race and the winner was Ch. Dress Circle Super Bee, owned by Robert and Jane Pruett. Thirty days later the National meeting took place at Macon, Georgia with a field of 42 adult starters. The high point winner, Volant's Big Red Machine (Gluhm), was having a very good season in 1973 and was one of the outstanding race Whippets of the year.

Volant's Big Red Machine had two other important victories this year. She was the high point winner in a field of 45 adults at the Tri-State Whippet Club meeting and at the Greater St. Louis Meeting over a field of 50. In the author's opinion this bitch is the best race Whippet whose height is within the Standard's limits since the great star of the early 1960's Eyeland Peppermint Boy.

The Tri-State meeting drew an additional 22 for the puppy races. These were won by Su Mic's Peaches and Cream (Wooten).

From the point of view of growth, quality of the dogs and overall enthusiasm of its patrons, Whippet racing in 1973 was in most excellent condition.

Marion Woodcock, a life-long supporter of the Whippet, passed away in January. She was the Secretary of the Whippet Association of California for many years, the first organized Whippet Club in the State.

This was the year that American registrations finally passed the thousand mark. The American Kennel Club processed 1,036 Whippet registrations for the year. During the same period the Kennel Club (England) had 1,869 added to its rolls.

1974

The year 1974 will probably be best remembered as the year the AWC held its first symposium. This was an all-day session that took place as part of the weekend program of the Midwest Specialty. The co-chairmen were Pat Dresser and Robert Pruett in charge of arrangements and Mrs. W. Potter Wear in charge of program. Speakers included Cora Miller on selection of show prospects and movement, JoAn Geise on training for the show ring, Roxanne Schaubhut on feeding for optimum development. Bernice Strauss and the Fred Saramentos gave a well-rounded obedience demonstration and the author with Gary Morgan presented the racing side of the picture. Finally Robert Theiss narrated a 30-minute film showing racing Whippets in action.

Attendance at the symposium and response to the program were excellent and the hope was expressed that this kind of program would become a regular feature of Whippet activities in every part of the country.

Ch. Winterfold's Bold Bid was still very much in evidence in the winners' circle at the beginning of the new year. She was William Brainard's choice for BB at Westminster over 41 other rivals. Mrs. Wear's Ch. Stoney Meadows Royal Flight was BOS.

At International the veteran all-breed judge Forest N. Hall passed on an entry of 30 and chose Ch. Coronation Golden Galileo, owned by Isabel Chamberlin as BB with Louis and Sene Auslander's Rimskittle Fool's Gold scoring BOS from the classes.

The Western Specialty was again held in conjuction with Santa Barbara. This weekend was really especially exciting in that Isabell Stoffers' Ch. Runner's Our Own Charisma got the nod for BB in a supported entry of 73 at Ventura under Mrs. John B. Patterson and from there was chosen best Hound under Mrs. Ramona Jones. She wrapped up the day with a thrilling BIS win over 3478 other dogs under J. D. Jones. She was handled to this great win by Mike Dougherty.

The Specialty itself had 108 entries with 98 present for British Judge R. M. James who made Ch. Highland Sea Chanty of Aani BB. Later the Specialty winner was GR3 to the eventual BIS winner under Anne Rogers Clark. The BOS came from American-bred dogs in the Colburns' Wheeling Gunsmoke. A Sweepstake was also held at the Western Specialty with the author judging. This competition drew 29 entries with Khivas Elizabeth Browning taking the top slot.

Ravenna was once again the scene of the Midwest Specialty. Patricia Speight was the judge and passed on 107 dogs. Ch. Misty Moor's Chalmondoley, owned by Roberta Russ, was BB and the well-known winner Ch. Mare's Head Royal Blu Princess, owned by JoAn Geise gained BOS. In the Sweepstakes Carousel's Canadian Caper, owned by Edward Jenner, was the best of the 44 entered.

For the East, the Specialty was held in conjunction with the Westbury KA show on Long Island. Norman Ellis made the trip from California to judge the 53 dogs and found his BB in the imported winner Ch. Charmoll Clansman. This steady campaigner from the Sporting Fields Kennels of Mr. and Mrs. James Butt scored a good GR2 later in the day under Margaret L. Walton. All through 1974 Clansman has been making good wins in strong competition and established himself as one of the nation's top win-

Ch. Runner's Our Own Charisma (Ch. Eyleland Double or Nothing ex Ch. Te-suque of Flying W), owned and bred by Isabell Stoffers, has the distinction of winning BIS over the largest all-breed entry ever won by a Whippet. This was at the Ventura County summer show in 1974 under J. D. Jones in a field of 3,478. A top winner she is shown in the ring by Michael Dougherty. *Roberts*.

Ch. Pennyworth I'm a Believer, owned by B. M. Johnson and J. Slater, BIS at the Willamette Valley Kennel Club show, 1974 under Mrs. C. Bede Maxwell. *Roberts*.

133

ners. Robert and Joan Goldstein had the BOS winner in their homebred, Gold-Dust's Twenty-Four Karat, a bitch that was to annex BB at Westminster's Centennial show 17 months into the future.

Silver State KC show in Las Vegas, Nevada was a supported show with a very full program. The annual meeting of the AWC took place here. The weekend also included a race meeting and a presentation by Roy Carlberg, AKC Vice-President.

Joan Frailey was the breed judge on this occasion and found 40 Whippets before her. It was another good day for Ch. Runner's Our Own Charisma who earned the right to go into the Hound Group. The Ladies' Dog Club in Massachusetts also received AWC support in 1974. Here Vincent Perry went over 39 Whippets and selected Joan Barlett's Ch. Bon Mot Gordo for BB. Gordo later went to the top of a good Hound Group under judge Harold Schlintz.

The year 1974 brought with it a full schedule of racing that yielded up a number of interesting results. Some new dogs caught the fancy's attention, some winners from 1973 kept up their strong pace and track stars of two years past were also in the news.

One of the new ones was Topper's Oh Golly Ms Molly (Thomas) who outpaced the best Western competition at the NCWC meeting at Fresno. A field of 32 starters were on hand. Another good turnout was present for the International meeting where 47 dogs raced in the feature. Antonio's Quick Silver (Maiullo) was undefeated for high point honors.

Van Oorschot's Toro, who made such good wins in 1973, continued buzzing by the competition. In 1974 he was the high point winner at the Great Western Spring meeting, all three Southern California meetings and the Ventura meeting held the weekend of the Western Specialty.

Epinard's Shelby of Wyndsor, a dog with an established track record and a high reputation was getting himself a piece of the action in this year. He was high point at the Northern California National race meeting at Santa Clara over 25 starters, the British Columbia race club meeting over 30 starters, the NCWFA meeting in San Jose over 51 others and the NCWC meeting in Fairfield defeating 50 rivals.

Epinard's Sonny Jim of Course was another who had many good races during 1974. He led the pack at the British Columbia group's Spring meeting in a field of 21 and at the Washington Whippet Racing Association meeting over 30 others.

The 1973 track star of the Midwest, Volant's Big Red Machine was still going strong in this year. Her victories included the Greater St. Louis meeting with 44 starters, the Champaign meeting with 53 and the Tri-State meeting with 44.

Other racers of note that came to attention in 1974 were Regalstock Lord Weasel O'Topper (Mathewson) who won the puppy races the day

Ch. Gold-Dust's Twenty Four Karat (Ch. Morshor's Bold N'Courageous ex Ch. Gold-Dust's All That Glitters), owned, and bred by Joan (handling) and Bob Goldstein, has made a number of impressive wins. She is shown taking BB at the Atlantic Whippet Assoc. supported entry at Brookhaven under Mrs. Fell. She was also BB at the 100th Westminster show under Mrs. Wear.

Bushman.

Dye-Or's Irish Crystal and Dye-Or's Irish Sparkle, top winning Whippet brace for 1974–75, owned, bred and handled by Don Dye. Shown scoring top honors at San Gabriel Valley under Winifred Heckmann, this pair has been Best Brace in Show 10 times to date. Both bitches also have show points and are accomplished racers. *Ludwig.*

135

before Santa Barbara and M. and M. of Course (Turpin, Jr.) winner of the British Columbia full meeting over 21 competitors.

Lure coursing was becoming an increasingly popular sport in California. The American Sighthound Field Association has been instrumental in the growth of the sport and offers championship certificates for dogs meeting the requirements for a coursing title. The first Whippet to earn a title in this department was Tiger Note of Keynote, CD while Betty Blalock's Zephyr, CD was the youngest Whippet to finish. He had his lure coursing title at 14 months. Epinard's Shelby of Wynsdor completed the requirements for his championship in three straight trials.

By 1974 Clare Hodge's Ch. Greenbrae Barn Dance had sired a total of 51 champions. Of this number, 15 were Group winners and some of these had Best in Show awards on their records. Barn Dance was the back cover model of the Christmas 1974 issue of the *Whippet News*. This issue, now a collector's item, was edited by Arnold Ross and Christine Cormany. The front cover model was the year's top winner Ch. Runner's Our Own Charisma.

Jeanne C. Henderson one of the breed's most respected veterans died in 1974 at the age of 86. Most memorable among her dogs were Ch. Home Place Shandygaff and Ch. Madcap Synidicated News.

The American Kennel Club registered 1,043 Whippets in 1974 and for the same period the Kennel Club (England) registered 2,088.

1975

By the mid-point of the 1970s the Whippet had become firmly established as one of America's prime exhibition breeds. A good Whippet is always a real threat in any Hound Group or Best in Show class and top wins for the breed are in no way unusual. Just as no one individual or kennel had dominated the awards in the breed, no one part of the country stands out as the prime area of Whippet activity. Good dogs and active breeders are now found wherever dogs are shown. And while the breed still is not thought of by the general public as the great housepet it is, the Whippet had definitely arrived and made a permanent place for itself in the world of show competition.

As usual Westminster attracted a top quality breed entry. Thelma Brown sorted out the winners in this year's gathering and came up with a pair of strong winners for the two top honors. Ch. Stoney Meadows Moon Mist was BB over 31 others while Ch. Bon Mot Gordo was BOS.

An entry of 31 was on hand at International and judge William Fetner found his BB in the open dog class. It was Marial's Kris Kringle, owned by the successful Strauss-Arthur team. Also in the Great Lakes area Ch. Charmoll Clansman was BB at two top shows. At Detroit he gained the

Ch. Madcap Syndicated News was one of the outstanding Whippets owned by Jeanne C. Henderson of Home Place Kennels. This was a great race Whippet as well as a top show dog, and to look at her one could easily determine she was built for the great speed she did deliver. *Ludwig*.

Batoka's Ziggy Stardust, owned and handled by Martha Fiedler, scoring a good win under breeder judge Isabell Stoffers at Pleasonton, California. *Francis*.

Ch. Stoney Meadows Moon Mist (Ch. Highlight's Eidolon ex Stoney Meadows Butterfly), owned by Mrs. Clare C. Hodge and bred by Mrs. Potter Wear, was the winner of numerous Hound Groups and was three times BIS. She was handled in the ring by Joy S. Brewster. *Klein.*

Ch. Charmoll Clansman (Maydale Cinnamon ex Dondelayo Ruanne), owned by Mr. and Mrs. James E. Butt and bred by Mrs. C. Dempster. A champion in England before importation, he has made an impressive string of wins in the United States including Groups and BIS at some of the most important affairs in the country. He is shown in the ring by Robert Forsyth. *Gilbert.*

nod for BB over 32 others from Howard Tyler and later under the same judge won a large, quality-filled Hound Group. At the Western Pennsylvania KA show he topped a breed entry of 18 under Melbourne Downing and went on to a good GR3 under Larry Downey.

The three 1975 AWC Specialties were the most successful in history. The West Coast Specialty was held, as usual, with Santa Barbara. There were two other all-breed shows held on the same weekend and all had large high-quality breed representation. The first show, held on the Friday, was the new Channel Cities Club affair. Here 61 Whippets came forward for Dr. William Houpt. Ch. Highland Sea Chanty of Aani was BB and later took GR3 under Helen Walsh. At Ventura Miss P. Batty judged 79 Whippets and sent the class bitch Cinnabar Backgammon, owned by N. and P. Rose into the Hound Group. At a show like Ventura the Groups are usually strong and the competition keen. This was the case here, but Backgammon brought in a GR3 under Mrs. Wear. This next day was the Specialty and Mrs. Wear judged. The 119 dogs present from an entry of 137 was a tremendous compliment to this veteran authority on the breed. When Mrs. Wear had finished her task Ch. Sheridan's Bianca, owned by Dr. John Shelton and Clifford Thompson, was the final winner. A class dog Highland Harka Cheyenne, owned by G. Kayhawn and D. Van Winkle was BOS. In the Hound Group, judged by the Australian authority, Graham Head, Bianca took a good second placing.

The Sweepstakes at Santa Barbara were judged by Kay Finch and her choice for best was Turfside's Butter Ripple, owned by Joe and Shirley Goss.

The Midwest Specialty came back to Ravenna in 1975 attracting an entry of 137 with 124 actually on hand for the opinion of Isabell Stoffers. Ch. Misty Moor's Chalmondeley was BB repeating his win of the previous year and Ch. Greyfriar Birdwatcher, owned by S. M. Sullivan was BOS. In Sweepstakes Cora Miller selected Jody of Whipoorwill, owned by Barbara Henderson and Deborah Wright as her best. Chalmondeley finished the day by taking a GR3 under Dr. Rex Foster. The next day, at the Chagrin Valley show Chalmondeley and Birdwatcher repeated their Specialty wins in an entry of 97 present under Graham Head.

Enterprise, the beautiful home of Mr. and Mrs. W. Potter Wear was the scene of the 1975 Eastern Specialty. Of an entry of 140, 116 were actually present on this important day for the breed. Gayle Gerber Bontecou made it two Specialty Bests in one year for Ch. Misty Moor's Chalmondeley and chose Ch. Gold-Dust's Twenty-Four Karat for BOS. The Sweepstake classes were judged by John Simm, a professional handler long associated with the dogs of the late Mrs. George Anderson and more recently with the Badgewood Hounds of Mrs. Fell. Out of an entry of 45 Mr. Simm chose Margaret Hodge's Highlight's Legacy for Best in Sweepstakes.

Ch. Misty Moor's Chalmondoley, owned by Roberta Russ, is a BIS winner and a multiple BB winner at the AWC Specialty. He is shown here going BB at the Chagrin Valley show under the Australian authority Graham Head, handler Jerry Edwards. *Ritter.*

Ch. Sheridan's Bianca, owned by Dr. John C. Shelton (handling) and Clifford W. Thompson, was BB under Mrs. Wear at the AWC Western Specialty. The show was held in conjunction with Santa Barbara and it drew a field of 119 competitors. Bianca was later Group second. *Bergman.*

141

Ch. Terrace Hills Bewitched, owned by Julie Holm and Joan Frailey (handling) had had a number of good Group and BIS wins. She is shown taking BIS at Antelope Valley under judge Robert Braithwaite. *Bergman*.

Mary Beth and Douglas Arthur with four homebreds. Their dogs compete regularly and successfully both on the track and in the show ring.

In 1975 Van Oorschot's Toro continued to lead the field in California races. He was undefeated during the year and is considered by many the top race Whippet of 1975. Other prominent Western race Whippets in 1975 were the great veteran Epinard's Shelby of Wyndsor, Lord Weasel O' Regalstock and Featherstone's Mr. Lightfoot.

In the Midwest Volant's Big Red Machine was still a standout, but the effects of age and a demanding career were beginning to show. She was heavily challenged by a number of speedy newcomers. With her, Knight Kap O'Lazebrook, Power of Destiny and Volant Buckeye Express were the standouts of Midwestern racing.

By 1975 52 dogs had won the AWC's Award of Racing Merit. It is hoped that this program will act as incentive to more Whippet fans to race their dogs and swell the ranks of the breed's honor roll. Ch. Pinetops' Opening Knight was now the leading sire of ARM holders with seven to date. This number should increase as time goes by.

Probably the most popular Whippet of 1975 was a dog that was neither a show winner nor a track star. Ashley Whippet, owned by Alex Stein and bred by the late Wally Schenck, makes a specialty of frisbee catching. He demonstrated his ability during the half-times of several important football games. National television audiences had the opportunity to see Ashley in action. Hopefully Ashley has, through his unique talent, made many new friends for the Whippet breed in America.

AKC registrations increased by only one over the previous year and as this is being written it would appear that numbers for 1976 will be close to the 1975 total of 1,044. The Kennel Club (England) processed 1,615 registrations for Whippets in 1975.

A group of Whippets on the bench at the Golden Gate show in San Francisico. Of the few benched shows left today, the California affairs usually present elaborately decorated benches tied in with a theme of the breed's function or country of origin.

Langdon.

The center of activities at Meander—the main house.

Two typical homebreds posing against the snow.

6

The Meander Story

Vᴇʀʏ ꜰᴇᴡ people had ever heard of Locust Dale, Virginia until Mr. George L. Shearer, an attorney from New York City, purchased historical Meander Farm and mansion built in the 1700s. Locust Dale in its entirety still consists of a combined general store and post office. Little did local Virginians realize, suffering through the early years of the Depression, that one tiny speck on the map midway between Culpepper and Orange would some day become known as "the home of the American-type Whippet." Much like the Whippet as a breed, growth in population around Locust Dale, Virginia has been slow.

It was not George Shearer who developed the American-type Whippet, but his two daughters, Julia and Judith. Both sisters remained unmarried during their entire lives, and were known by local Virginians from Washington, D. C. to Richmond as Miss Julia and Miss Judith.

The Shearer Sisters

My lifelong friendship with Julia and Judy Shearer started when I was thirteen years old and we remained close friends for the rest of their lives. The many days and weeks I spent at Meander over the years, and our many visits to dog shows, horse sales, buying trips for fish, birds, and other pets are among the most cherished memories of my life. This close relationship for forty years was more of a family relationship, as both sis-

145

ters often remarked in later years, "They had known me since the days I wore diapers."

Julia and Judy Shearer had an outstanding knowledge of livestock. They hated chickens, but did raise game cocks for me during two years of World War II when it was necessary for me to give up my animals. While the Shearer sisters were very similar in many ways, each owned her own dogs, horses, etc. One sister did not attempt to run the life of the other when it came to their personal animals and pets. It was always very easy for me to communicate with Julia and Judy on an individual basis. I learned very early in our friendship that while they were often called the Shearer sisters, they demanded individual attention and respect. There were many occasions in my life when they went to bat for me as a team. Julia and Judy Shearer did not accumulate a great number of close friends in their lifetime. They did, however, receive great respect from all who knew them for their knowledge and ability to produce quality dogs, horses, cattle and hogs.

Judith Shearer was the younger sister. She devoted her entire life to Meander Whippets and seldom left the farm except to attend shows, short shopping trips and a few visits with personal friends. Judy worked in the kennel and supervised the daily kennel operations. Labor was often a great problem at Meander, so if no help was available, Judy would handle the kennel alone. The one major trip she took in her life was a judging assignment to England and Scotland accompanied by Mrs. Augustus (Adelaide) Riggs IV. Judith Shearer had a better eye for Whippets than her sister Julia, and was also responsible for the operation of the home.

Julia Shearer was the business head of Meander Farm. She disliked cooking and housework as much as she did chickens. Julia was more interested in hogs, cattle, and thoroughbred horses than was sister Judy, and had great success in most of her livestock ventures. During the last ten years of her life, most of her time was spent raising and selling thoroughbred horses. Several Meander-bred colts earned over $100,000 each on the track in purse money. Demand for Meander-bred yearlings was great. One year, Meander topped the Keenland Fall Yearling Sales, Lexington, Kentucky. This was a first for a breeder not living in Kentucky. The most successful brood mare for Meander was Vital and Degage was the best producing stallion. It was not until the 1950s that Julia Shearer showed interest in horse racing. Her early success of the 1930s and 1940s was with hunter-jumpers. Substitution and Mathematician were her best and brought the highest prices of any of the hunter-jumpers developed and sold by Meander. Dewey Clatterburk started with Meander in the 1930s and was stable manager for Meander up until Julia Shearer passed away.

Julia Shearer gave me my first race horse soon after World War II. This was a two-year-old filly named Lucky Penny. At that time, I never ex-

```
                              Mathew of Sion Hill      Flick of Oxon
                                                       Eleanor
              Sandblaze
                              Gracie's Pet             Ch. Willesbeaux
                                                       Lindy Loo
  Ch. Sandbrilliant of Meander
                              Stopwheel                Pentamar Stopper
                                                       Flywheel
              Tregear Fascination
                              Carn Brea Lassie         Pinea Swift
                                                       Queenie
CH. MICA OF MEANDER
                              Ch. Coolridge Flying Fury  Ch. Freemanor Glencoe Supreme
                                                          Margie Cameo
              Kissell's Buddie
                              Patricia                 Ch. Freemanor Glencoe Supreme
                                                       Ch. Iansdown First Flight
  Ch. Syndicate of Meander
                              Towyside Smoke           Ch. Manorley Maori
                                                       Girl Scout
              Ch. Towyside Teasle
                              Towyside Tingle          Watford Bon
                                                       Watford Myrth
```

Ch. Mica of Meander was the Shearers' top show dog and producing sire.

```
                              Manorley Manala          Iashaway
                                                       Harlow Heroine
        Samema Snowflight
                              Oxted Dainty Maid        Tiptree George
                                                       Avonhill Pride
  Ch. Oldown Stormy
                              Downtrooper              Ch. Boy Scrounger
                                                       Sandbronze
        Oldown True Love
                              Downtitania              Downtrooper
                                                       Sandbrandy
CH. DIZZY BLOND OF MEANDER
                              Ch. Mica of Meander      Ch. Sandbrilliant of Meander
                                                       Ch. Syndicate of Meander
        Ch. Ptarmigan of Meander
                              San Benito Flash         Ch. Zanza Zoco of V
                                                       Corsian Winsome One
  Question of Meander
                              Ch. Nimbus of Meander    Ch. Mica of Meander
                                                       Sunshine of Althea
        Windholme Cloudy
                              Ch. Quiz of Meander      Ch. Sandbrilliant of Meander
                                                       Fortune's Test of Meander
```

Ch. Dizzy Blond of Meander, in the opinion of the Shearer Sisters, Meander's best
producing bitch after the original Sanbrilliant/Syndicate cross.

Sunnysand O'Iazeland   Ch. Carbon Copy of Meander
Ch. Clytie of Meander

Ch. Picardia Fieldfare

Ch. Picardia Polka Dot   Ch. Tiptree Noel
Ch. Frosty Morn of Meander

Ch. Meander Robin

Ch. Meander Man of Letters   Ch. Mica of Meander
Meander Pickaninny

Scarlet Letter of Meander

Hunter's Moon of Meander   Windholme Sandstorm
Windholme Patricia

CH. MEANDER BOBWHITE

Samema Snowflight   Manorley Manala
Oxted Dainty Maid

Ch. Oldown Stormy

Oldown True Love   Downtrooper
Downtitania

Ch. Dizzy Blond of Meander

Ch. Ptarmigan of Meander   Ch. Mica of Meander
San Benito Flash

Question of Meander

Windholme Cloudy   Ch. Nimbus of Meander
Ch. Quiz of Meander

Ch. Meander Bobwhite was Meander's top show dog during the 1960s.

Ch. Sandbrilliant of Meander   Sandblaze
Tregear Fascination

Ch. Mica of Meander

Ch. Syndicate of Meander   Kissell's Buddie
Ch. Towyside Teasle

Ch. Meander Man of Letters

Ch. Zanza Zoco of V   Zanza Zagreb
Zanza Zanita

Meander Pickaninny

Corsian Winsome One   Ch. Pocon's Jewel's Dawn
Ch. Demi Tasse

CH. MEANDER COPPERPLATE

Flick of Ups and Downs   Ch. Clansman of Ups and Downs
Ch. Cindy of Ups and Downs

Ch. Son of Flick

Shu Fly   Heelfly
Touch and Out of Meander

Princess De Anna

Ch. Silver Image   Ch. Meander Graven Image
Ch. Quicksilver of Meander

Happy Birthday of Kingston

Pride of Kingston   Ch. Pegram's Red Wagon
Patchwork of Meander

Ch. Meander Copperplate represents, on the dam's side, the greatest cross of
combination race/show Whippets bred by Meander. Ch. Pegram's Red Wagon was
Meander's best race Whippet and his son, Heelfly, was the top racer of his day.
Ch. Clansman of Ups and Downs was a full brother to Red Wagon from another mating.

pected to have enough money to own and race horses. Lucky Penny did not win and was claimed from me at the Charlestown, West Virginia track for $800. This was my start in horse racing which has been a continuing part of my life.

The Breeding Program

After the highly successful mating of Ch. Sandbrilliant of Meander to Ch. Syndicate, common-sense matings, using outstanding individuals backed up by winning pedigrees made Meander the most successful kennel in America. Ch. Mica of Meander and his get carried on best in early Meander bloodlines. There were so many good and great Whippets bred by Meander from 1930 to 1955 that no one Meander-bred stud or brood bitch was used to establish greatness as an individual producer.

A review of Meander pedigrees through the years would indicate that the bitch, Dizzy Blond of Meander by Ch. Oldown Stormy out of Question of Meander was more successful in Meander pedigrees than any other dog since Mica. Ch. Meander Bob White and Ch. Meander Mockingbird were probably two of the best dogs shown by Meander in later years. Ch. Meander Bob White still appears in many pedigrees of top quality show Whippets, but he could not be considered a truly great sire. Dizzy Blond of Meander, however, appears in a large number of pedigrees of dogs that had great success on both the track and in the show ring. The source of racing desire and ability seems to stem from Lorelei O'Lazeland, a daughter of Dizzy Bond. While most dogs carrying Lorelei O'Lazeland in their pedigrees have a great desire to run the lure, her best producers of combination show and racing Whippets were the littermates, Ch. Legend O'Lazeland and Ch. Rouget O'Lazeland.

The Kennel

The first kennels at Meander in 1930 were large pens with dog houses or sheds in each pen. Distemper and hookworm took a heavy toll in pure-bred dogs at that time. Meander had more than its share of problems over the years until modified live virus vaccine was developed by Cornell University some 25 years later. In the mid 1930's a new cinder block kennel was built. The kennel had twenty inside units with small outside runs, a kitchen, a very large grooming room with small outside runs, another very large grooming room with holding cages and a hall area that was the reception room for the kennel. A kennel warming was held when the new Meander kennel building was completed, and many prominent dog and horse people came from great distances for the kennel opening. The buffet was professionally catered in the kennel, with tables in each of the

149

twenty inside kennel units. The kennel was later explanded with a separate cinder block puppy house. This building had four very large indoor units with outside runs. A bit later, six pens were built on concrete and equipped with large dog houses. These were used for developing growing puppies once they left the puppy house. The original dirt run pens were retained and the dogs were allowed to exercise daily in these pens when housed in the main kennel unit. During the mid 1960s, age and health became a problem for both Julia and Judy. Meander Whippets did not get to use the big runs on a set pattern. Consequently, problems in temperament and flat feet increased.

Meander registered over 150 litters of Whippets during its years of operation. The average kennel population at Meander ran from 35 to 70. This included old Whippets, puppies and house pets. There were usually puppies at Meander, and many were for sale. In fact, Julia and Judy Shearer made most of their stock available for sale. Meander did not advertise, but unless one was considered an enemy, and would pay the price asked, a prospective customer could buy a Meander-bred Whippet of his liking.

Meander and the Racing Scene

The Misses Shearer did not dislike Whippet racing as much as many were led to believe or wanted to believe. I raced Meander Whippets off and on for forty years, many times on a partnership basis with Julia or Judy. Whippet racing in America is heavily represented by Meander Whippets or Meander bloodlines in all sections of the country where Whippet racing has been conducted. Julia and Judy Shearer did not feel they personally could compete in Whippet racing. Both sisters fully realized that the racing of Whippets as carried on in America was not conducted "by little boys wearing short pants." They were confident that their better Whippets could compete with great success in racing. Both Shearer sisters were, in their own way, shrewd traders in dogs. They wanted their bloodlines and individual dogs in the hands of those who could win and add prestige to their kennel. Whippet racing was not a lady's game in the 1930s and 1940s, so Meander Kennels bred them, and those of us in the business of racing Whippets did the training.

The Shearers and the AWC

Julia and Judy Shearer changed in many ways between 1930 and 1970. The same was true of the types of Whippets that represented Meander. In 1934 the Shearer sisters took over the American Whippet Club paying off

For many years most Meander Whippets were either red or fawn and had outstanding personality and courage.

Most of the Meanders were kennel dogs, but the domain of the house Whippets was the living room couch.

A view of the first single-unit kennel building at Meander. It was built during the late 1930s. *Courtesy American Kennel Club.*

Over the years Meanders changed in type but not in elegance. This is Meander Ten Four with Judith Shearer.

One of the last Meander studs was Meander Hindsight who was used during the latter half of the 1960s to keep down height. He is shown here with Judith Shearer.

the borrowed money, approximately $100 that had kept the Club in existence during the early years of Depression. The American Whippet Club was run virtually as a private Eastern organization until increased national interest in Whippets started soon after World War II. The Shearers did an excellent job operating the American Whippet Club, controlling the breed Standard and operating one Eastern Specialty Show each year. There was no doubt that both Julia and Judy felt that the American Whippet Club was theirs for many years.

Both sisters were very jealous of the Whippet Breeders Association of Maryland. This organization was the real power among American Whippet owners, not the very limited, active membership of the American Whippet Club. There were many periods from 1935 to 1946 when my trying to keep both organizations on speaking terms was difficult. The Whippet was such a numerically small breed, and this was especially true of registered Whippets in America. The AKC registered only 54 Whippets in 1930, 77 in 1940 and 89 in 1950. It was absolutely necessary to have a working agreement between the Whippet Breeders Association of Maryland and the American Whippet Club to even keep the Whippet in existence.

The author's personal friendship with Julia and Judy did much to keep open conflict at a minimum. Julia Shearer and I visited the American Kennel Club regarding registration of Whippets in America. Many registrations lapsed during the years of the depression, and the officials of the American Whippet Club agreed to open the stud book for a limited period. All Whippets accepted by the American Kennel Club without registration were approved both by Julia Shearer and the author. This helped to some extent, but interest in registered Whippets was still very limited. The Whippet Breeders Association of Maryland carried a stud book and listed more dogs than did the American Kennel Club at that time.

With the discontinuing of local option betting after World War II, the Whippet Breeders Association of Maryland eventually dissolved. The showing of Whippets was now becoming the major Whippet interest. New fanciers began to challenge the established Eastern kennels for national supremacy in the show ring. The American Whippet Club experienced a struggle for power and prestige in the breed. Julia and Judith Shearer tried desperately to keep the Club as it existed in the mid 1930s. But times had changed, as had many of the fancy. By the mid 1960s the Shearer sisters had virtually withdrawn from all American Whippet Club activities, taking with them some resentment of the changed attitude of the Whippet fancy.

Part of the collection of books and bronzes the Shearer sisters bequeathed to the American Kennel Club.

Courtesy American Kennel Club.

The bronze of Ch. Mica of Meander and his championship certificate, from the Shearer Collection at the American Kennel Club.

Courtesy American Kennel Club.

154

The big mansion on the hill at Meander Farms surrounded by massive boxwood bushes was a virtual fortress of security for the Shearer sisters. They operated virtually in isolation at Meander Farms both in victory and in defeat. As showing and breeding became more competitive, they gradually dropped out of major show ring competition. Both sisters were excellent handlers, but spent little time in breaking their Whippets to leash. In the early days,if you posed your Whippet well, movement had very little meaning. The Shearers always handled their own Whippets, and as moving a Whippet in the ring became more important, Julia and Judy became less effective in winning as did Meander Whippets on the whole. Notwithstanding, dogs handled by Julia and Judy Shearer won over fifty championships. Most of these victories came in the days when there was a limited number of dog shows. This was an extremely outstanding record based on the conditions of the time.

Whippets fell in two categories at Meander; house Whippets known as "people dogs," or kennel Whippets who seldom left their quarters except for occasional visits to shows. Both Shearer sisters preferred males to females as a general rule, thus, the house dog population at Meander usually consisted of males. Judy was devoted to a Whippet named "Nora" who had a broken right front leg. Nora and a little English male named Mickey (Oldown Panda), were her two favorite pets. Julia generally selected her better males for house pets. Personality was the factor with Meander house dogs, not necessarily conformation.

As Julia Shearer became more interested in thoroughbred horses and Angus cattle, Meander Whippets became almost the entire responsibility of Judith Shearer. Judy had a bad fall from a horse in the early 1930s, leaving her with a cast in one eye and a rather stiff neck. She did not enjoy the best of health in later life. And, eventually this reflected in the temperament and type of dogs that had made Meander famous in the 1930s and 1940s.

The Decline of Meander

The well-defined Ch. Sandbrilliant—Ch. Syndicate family who crossed so very well with other families used in making Meander Whippets "the number one type in America," began to change in appearance in many cases. Julia and Judy felt bitches did not usually make good house pets, thus they were left in the kennel. As time went on, shyness and sour disposition began to crop up. The solid colors that marked early Meander greats gave way to white ground color. With this came a change in the appearance of Meander type, with fronts becoming narrower, and in some cases, high, hackney movement, not typical of the early, low, free-moving fawns, reds and brindles, all with very dark eyes. The consistently good, often cat-footed, Meanders gave way to dogs with longer toes, splay feet and long pasterns. It is my feeling that lack of exercise and living in concrete runs during puppyhood was at least part of the reason for the foot problem. Testicle problems in males began to show heavily in some breedings. Excellent pigmentation and elegant appearance always remained a part of Meander Whippets, until the kennel was discontinued.

Meander kennels culled more heavily than any Whippet kennel in America. When Judy enjoyed normal health and was campaigning regularly, much time was given to developing young stock. In later years, some knowledgeable Whippet breeders felt that pups were discarded too soon and that many of the better Meander Whippets never were allowed to reach maturity.

Conditions changed radically at Meander during the late 1960s with the decline in health of both Julia and Judy. Their passing signalled the end of an era. To me and to those who knew Julia and Judy Shearer and Meander Whippets through the years, there could be no question as to this combination of women and dogs having the greatest positive influence on the Whippet in America. No matter how you pronounce the words Shearer and Meander, the spelling will always be W-H-I-P-P-E-T.

Judith R. Shearer and Fayetta Julia Shearer bequeathed all of their dog books, paintings and bronzes to the American Kennel Club. The Shearer Collection remains in the custody of the American Kennel Club at this time. Meander Kennels rightfully remain the true foundation of the modern Whippet in America.

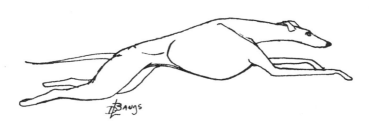

7

The English Influence

First generation crosses of English imports on already established American and English-American families are a major factor in the Whippets seen today in the American show ring. The past 10 years would show a strong trend toward the first generation English-American cross, with the decline in the American type. Meander, Stoney Meadows, Eyleland, Whippoo, Lazeland, Renfield, Garden City, Hollyparke, Traymatt, Great Circle, Home Place, and a number of smaller West Coast breeders all favored the larger, American type at one time. Yet, it would be very difficult to prove that the influence of English imports crossed on American Whippets is not a greater factor in producing quality show Whippets, than mating established American lines and families with each other.

Direct English imports have been important to the development of the all-around Whippet since the breed first came to America. Whippets bred by Manorley and Shirley Kennels, followed by W. L. Beara with the Willes Strain, and Bernard S. Fitter of Boy Scrounger and Snooker fame, figure heavily in Whippets bred by such American pioneers as Arthur Rankin, Elsah Voss, Mae Bland, Amy L. Bonham, George D. White, Blanche Haring, Harry E. Damon, Jr., Freeman Ford, Felix Angus Leser, McClure Halley and E. Coe Kerr.

During the Depression years of the 1930s and the recovery years prior to World War II, English imports still played a major role in American Whippets. The most famous of the Shearer matings was the breeding of

English Ch. Laguna Ligonier has had tremendous impact on the breed in America through a number of the imports he has sired. Both show winners and track stars can trace back to him. Among his many excellent progeny was the fine winner and producer, Ch. Greenbrae Barn Dance. *Cooke.*

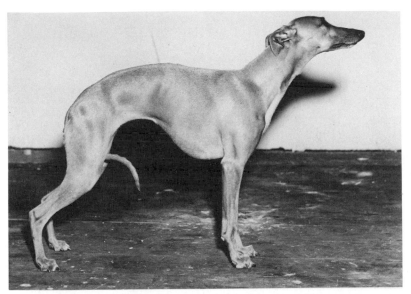

Ch. Greenbrae Laguna Lucia, a top winner and producer in Great Britain. *Cooke.*

Ch. Samarkand's Greenbrae Tarragon, one of Britain's all-time top winners and producers. *Cooke.*

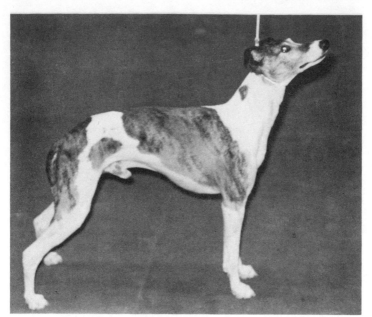

Ch. Tantivity Diver, imported and first owned in America by Margaret P. Newcombe, was a most beneficial influence to American bloodlines. He was later acquired by Mrs. and Mrs. Charles Billings with whom he spent the remainder of his life.

This is one of England's top race Whippets. In spite of his color, he is named Blackie and is by Golden Wyne ex Blue Fawn. Owned by Mr. and Mrs. Ken Arnold, he is raced extensively in the Yorkshire vicinity. *Smallwood.*

the two English dogs Ch. Sandbrilliant of Meander to Ch. Syndicate of Meander. All offspring in turn produced quality individuals and were the real foundation of Meander and the American type. Other English imports who helped establish Meander as the premier Whippet kennel in America were Ch. Tiptree Noel and Ch. Oldown Stormy. Oldown Panda, purchased at a later date, did not cross well with the then established Meander bloodlines.

Second only to Meander Kennels in size, number of Whippets, and show record was the beautiful Mardomere Kennels owned by Mrs. Margaret Hubbs Anderson. Mrs. Anderson built her kennel on English imports and English brood stock. The major factors in the success of Mardomere were dogs from Stanley Wilkins of Tiptree Kennel fame. Laguna Whippets were strongly represented at Mardomere, as were numerous other English imports purchased for Mrs. Anderson by Percy Roberts and other astute dog men. Many fanciers of the period often spoke of Mardomere as an English Whippet kennel located in America.

Prominent today in American bloodlines are English Whippets who came from Ladiesfield Kennels owned by Mrs. Margaret Wiggs, Benachie Kennels owned by Mr. and Mrs. Donald Gollan, Of Test Kennels owned by Mrs. Dorothy Lewis (who was even better known in Greyhounds) and Poppy Kennels owned by Mrs. Eileen Martin. Most familiar English Kennels to American Whippet breeders are the Allways Kennels owned by Mr. and Mrs. Fred Jones, Laguna Kennels owned by Mrs. D. U. McKay and the Wingedfoot Kennels owned by Mr. C. H. Douglas Todd. Dondelayo bloodlines are also producing many outstanding winners in the American show ring. As one closely reviews the heavy influence of the English Whippet on American bloodlines and families, they must quickly realize there probably would not be an American-type Whippet were it not for the direct influence of English imports.

Credit for producing the greatest number of top winning show Whippets in America can be traced directly to Eng. Ch. Bellavista Barry. The major sources of his influence on American Whippets comes from his sons, Eng. Ch. Laguna Ligonier, Eng. and Am. Ch. Courtenay Fleetfoot of Pennyworth and his half brother, Eng. and Am. Ch. Ringmore Finisterre. Ch. Courtenay Fleetfoot of Pennyworth was particularly successful in producing outstanding combination race and show Whippets.

Ch. Laguna Ligonier's impact on the breed is strongest through Ch. Greenbrae Barn Dance brother to Am. and Can. Ch. Coveydown Greenbrae Wayfarer. Ch. Greenbrae Barn Dance carries on best through his great producing son, Ch. Morshor's Whirlaway. Eng. and Am. Ch. Tantivity Diver, another producing son of Ligonier, has sired outstanding combination show and race Whippets. His best producing son of combination show and race Whippets is Ch. Pennyworth Would You Believe.

The extended, inbred pedigree of Ch. Morshor's Whirlaway clearly shows the great influence of Ch. Bellavista Barry (third and fourth generations). The major carrier of the Barry line is Ch. Greenbrae Barn Dance (first and second generations) followed by Ch. Laguna Ligonier (second and third generations) with the fine producing bitch, Ch. Greenbrae Laguna Lucia (second and third generations) followed by Ch. Laguna Leading Lady and Ch. Lilly of Laguna who both appear in Whirlaway's third and fourth generations.

```
                                                              Ch. Pilot Officer Prune
                              Ch. Bellavista Barry            Brekin Bright Spark
              Ch. Laguna Ligonier
                                                              Ch. Fieldspring Bartsia of Allways
                              Ch. Lilly of Laguna             Ch. Brekin Ballet Shoes
      Ch. Greenbrae Barn Dance
                                                              Allways Wingedfoot Running Fox
                              Ch. Runaway Controller          Evening Mist
              Ch. Greenbrae Laguna Lucia
                                                              Ch. Bellavista Barry
                              Ch. Laguna Leading Lady         Ch. Lilly of Laguna

CH. MORSHOR'S WHIRLAWAY
                                                              Ch. Bellavista Barry
                              Ch. Laguna Ligonier             Ch. Lilly of Laguna
              Ch. Greenbrae Barn Dance
                                                              Ch. Runaway Controller
                              Ch. Greenbrae Laguna            Ch. Laguna Leading Lady
                                         Lucia
      Ch. Hill's Harvest Moon Dance
                              Solar System O'Lazeland         American Breeding
                                                              American Breeding
              Seven League Snowscape
                                                              American Breeding
                              Ch. Seven League Songbird       American Breeding
```

8

The Whippet in Canada

THE RELATIONSHIP between most American and Canadian Whippet owners is very close, it is often difficult to realize that there are boundaries between the two countries. This relationship started in the 1920s and covers all phases of breeding, showing and racing. Certainly the good neighbor policy between the USA and Canada applies to the Whippet Fancy.

Whippets bred and exhibited in Canada are registered by the Canadian Kennel Club while Whippets bred and exhibited in the USA are registered by the American Kennel Club. These two registration bodies recognize each others' registrations, but when dogs are transferred across the border permanently, registration must be transferred to the country of the applicable governing body. The Canadian Kennel Club has slightly different show rules and regulations, thus points accumulated for championships in Canada do not count in the USA and the same is true of Whippets going from the USA to Canada. Many Whippets, however, do have both American and Canadian championships. Canada, much like the USA, has a very small Whippet population, thus it is very easy to identify most of the Whippet owners in Canada. Canadian breeders probably import more from England than from the USA. In many cases, American and Canadian pedigrees are very similar, and dogs from both countries have pedigrees very heavy in English bloodlines.

Canadian Fanciers

There are probably more Whippets in Eastern Canada than in British Columbia. Working relationships with American breeders relating to dual purpose Whippets is greater between the show-race groups from British Columbia than is the case with those who only show their Whippets and live in the Toronto area. Mrs. Joyce Anson and her daughter, Pamela, moved from England to Aldergrove, British Columbia. As a mother-daughter kennel, their efforts met with immediate success both in the show ring and in racing. Their two foundation bitches, English imports, Prudence of Conevan and Can. Ch. Rockabye Peace Pipe were both successful brood matrons. The breeding of Tinribs Tiger Rag to Ch. Peace Pipe started the famous Sonna line for Mrs. Anson and the Rockabye family for Pamela Arthur, now married. Peace Pipe in her first litter produced three champion daughters in Rockabye Black Mollie, Pandy and Gypsy. Ch. Rockabye Gypsy, produced the outstanding Can. and Am. Ch. Gypsy's Kelly, CD, one of the outstanding racers in British Columbia and along the Pacific Coast. Kelly, bred back to Ch. Rockabye Black Mollie produced the Group winning litter of Ch. Sonna Bambi and Can. and Am. Ch. Sonna Rockabye Baby. Rockabye Baby was the winner of the American Whippet Club national race meeting, Santa Barbara, California, and was the top racer in Canada in 1963. Sonna and Rockabye bloodlines continue to produce top quality show and race Whippets.

Following in the footsteps of Mrs. Joyce Anson and Pamela Arthur, were Mr. and Mrs. Richard Webster, Urray Kennels, also of British Columbia. From the mid 1960s to the early 1970s Urray Whippets were outstanding in the show ring and in Whippet racing. Original brood stock included Ch. Rockabye Calamity Jane O'Urray, Can. and Am. Ch. Stars and Stripes of Suntan, CD and Hollypark Baby Doll. Outstanding race and show Whippets bred by Urray kennels were Ch. Urray Diamond Lill, Ch. Urray Kateydid, Ch. Urray Wild Bill, Urray Chieftan, Urray Be Bad Boy, Urray Quick Nick. Ch. Urray Speed Queen, owned by Mrs. Ann Whitton, was the first Whippet to complete her UD degree in Canada.

Perhaps the greatest Canadian influence on Whippet racing in America was the entrance of William Turpin, Sr., William Turpin, Jr., and their families into the breeding and racing of Whippets in British Columbia and in all sections of the USA where Whippet racing is held. The Turpin family uses the affix "of Course," and produces the type Whippet that fits well in the show ring and on the race track, most having outstanding temperament. William Turpin, Sr. and Jr. are also the major force behind Whippet racing in British Columbia as conducted under Official Rules and Regulations for National Whippet Racing, approved by The American Whippet Club.

Some of the best known Whippets owned by the Turpin family are

The Turpins and their Whippets have played a great part in popularizing the breed in the show ring and on the track in Canada. Shown here (from left) are William Turpin, Jr. with Renfield Temptress of Course and Emberson of Course, William Turpin, Sr. with Epinard's Sonny Jim of Course and the elder Turpin's grandson with Rockabye Ember of Course. All these dogs have completed their show championships and have earned the Award of Racing Merit certificate.

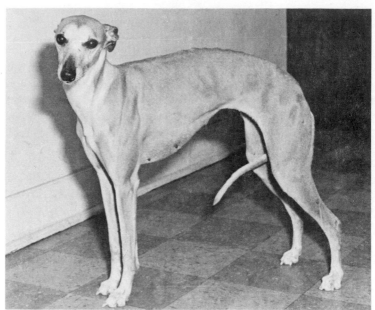

Canadian Ch. Rockabye Ember of Course, ARM, was an outstanding race and show Whippet. She added to this by producing well and is in the pedigrees of many dual-purpose animals in Canada and in the United States.

Canadian Ch. Epinard's Sonny Jim of Course (Canadian Ch. Emberson of Course ex Eyleland Hannah) was a prominent track star on both sides of the border.

Can. Ch. Rockabye Ember of Course, ARM (Pennyworth Tumbleweed ex Can. & Am. Ch. Sonna Rockabye Baby CD), Can. Ch. Emerson of Course, ARM (Can. & Am. Ch. Stars and Stripes of Suntan C D ex Can. Ch. Rockabye Ember of Course, ARM), Can. Ch. Strip Tease of Course (Can. & Am. Ch. Stars and Stripes of Suntan ex Can. Ch. Rockabye Ember of Course, ARM). Strip Tease was a Specialty winner and her brother Sonny was a Group winner. Can. Ch. Renfield Temptress of Course, ARM (Eyleland Homer ex Can. Ch. Rockabye Ember of Course, ARM) and Can. Ch. Epinard's Sonny Jim of Course, ARM (Can. Ch. Emberson of Course, ARM ex Eyleland Hannah) are two more of the Turpins fine dogs.

Before leaving British Columbia we must include Mr. and Mrs. Pearl Baumgartner and daughter, Carol, White Acres Kennel, Puyallup, Washington. The Baumgartners are mentioned many times in connection with their tremendous constructive influence on American Whippet racing on the West Coast. The Baumgartner family, while living in the USA, made many important contributions to the expansion of Whippet racing in British Columbia.

One of the key influences in the production of top show Whippets in Eastern Canada was the move of Colonel and Mrs. John Collings, Winterfold Kennels, from England to America and then to Canada. Ch. Winterfold Bold Bid, was one of the top-winning show Whippets in America, and a producing brood bitch. Sean M. Sullivan and the Birdwatcher Whippets make their presence felt in stateside show rings. Ch. Dondelayo Buccaneer owned by Max Magder, Toronto, is a consistent winner, and has a Best in Show in the United States. The Whippet Club of Eastern Canada is organizing many activities to create greater interest in the dual Whippet at this writing, and Americans are most fortunate to have such a good Whippet neighbor across the border.

9

The American Whippet Club

THE AMERICAN Whippet Club is a member club of the American Kennel Club. It is the parent club of the breed, and a non-profit organization. The major functions of the American Whippet Club are:

1. Development and maintenance of the breed Standard, the guideline in words by which Whippets are judged on conformation.
2. The responsibility of developing programs and operating under the club constitution and by-laws. The objectives of the American Whippet Club are:
   A. To unite those people interested in breeding, showing, racing, coursing and generally improving the Whippet for the purpose of effectively exerting a combined influence upon all matters affecting the breed.
   B. To urge members and breeders to accept the Standard of the breed as approved by the American Kennel Club as the only standard of excellence by which the Whippet shall be judged.
   C. To promote and maintain a high standard of conduct in transaction of all business connected with the breeding of Whippets.
   D. To conduct sanctioned matches, obedience trials and Specialty shows held under the rules of the American Kennel Club.
3. Prepare Official Rules and Regulations for National Whippet Racing.

Present Award of Racing Merit Certificates to those outstanding race Whippets who accumulate fifteen or more Award of Racing Merit points in officially approved race meetings held under Official Rules and Regulations for National Whippet Racing. Operation of approved Whippet race meetings are carried out by local AWC members who request permission to operate an official meeting.

Changes in the Whippet Standard and the constitution and by-laws require a two-thirds favorable vote by membership in good standing. Changes in Official Rules and Regulations for National Whippet Racing require a majority vote of the nine-man Board of Directors. Three Board members come up for reelection every year. Term of office for a Board member is three years, but Board members can be reelected for more than one three-year term.

Membership is open to persons over eighteen years of age who are in good standing with the American Kennel Club and subscribe to the purpose of the American Whippet Club. An applicant for membership should be an owner and/or breeder of Whippets for at least two years. An applicant must fill out a questionnaire on his or her background in Whippets. Application is then reviewed by Board of Directors of AWC and requires a three-fourths favorable vote of the directors at said meeting.

The first available records on American Whippet Club activities start with 1930. Records during the period 1930 through 1934 are extremely vague with a very high turnover of officers and membership. The early Depression years of the 1930s created great financial problems for those who had been active in the Whippet fancy prior to 1930. Total membership at the time was less than twenty.

From 1935 through 1945 the American Whippet Club operated effectively as a small group under the leadership of the Misses Julia and Judith Shearer, Mr. Harry Peters, Jr. and Mr. Edward T. Nash. Numerous members and officers during this period were prominent in purebred dog activities, but their actual interest in Whippets was extremely limited. Major emphasis by the American Whippet Club during this 10-year period was the operation of one major Specialty show held in a location most convenient to the majority of Whippet owners living in the East.

The period 1946 through 1953 was one of close association between the American Whippet Club and the Greyhound Club of America. Mr. William Brainard and Mr. James A. Farrell, both extremely active in Greyhounds and Fox Terriers, acted as officers of the American Whippet Club at times during this period. These two Parent Clubs often held joint specialties. Membership grew only slightly during these years with emphasis on one major Eastern Specialty each year and donations to other worthy causes.

The period 1954 through 1960 saw the American Whippet Club begin moving from an Eastern organization towards recognizing the needs of the Whippet nationally. During this period the Board of Directors was increased from seven to nine members. The Board members now included individuals living in other than the Eastern part of the country. The annual Eastern Specialty concept was expanded so there was an American Whippet Club Specialty held in the East, the Midwest and on the West Coast. The Constitution and By-Laws were also slightly altered to better cover the constant increase in Whippet population and ownership in all parts of America.

The *Whippet News*

The *Whippet News*, official publication of the American Whippet Club, was started in 1956 under the editorship of Louis Pegram, who, after one year, turned the responsibility over to Mrs. Eugene Jacobs. Whippet racing again became a major interest with many members of the American Whippet Club. The first successful race meeting since the 1940s was held at the International Kennel Club Show, Chicago, Illinois. The American Whippet Club Board of Directors was divided for several years in recognizing Whippet racing, as the American Kennel Club does not support racing of any type. Most of the people racing Whippets at this time were members of the American Whippet Club, and many of the dogs participating in racing had finished their championships in the show ring. After three years of study and debate, the Board of Directors approved Louis Pegram to draw up Official Rules and Regulations for National Whippet Racing, leaving the supervision of these rules to various groups of members who wished to take part.

A Growing Club

The true expansion period of the American Whippet Club was from 1960 to the present. The membership exceeded 200 by the end of 1970. A new Constitution and By-Laws were drawn up and approved by the American Kennel Club. The program of approved Parent Specialties was expanded to three regional affairs of equal importance, and up to nine AWC supported entry shows. *The Whippet News*, official publication of the AWC, moved to California under the editorship of Christine Cormany.

From 1970 through 1975 the membership of the American Whippet Club voted for slight changes and clarification in the Whippet Standard to include the following disqualifications:

1. Blue or china colored eyes.
2. Undershot or overshot mouth one-quarter inch or more.
3. A dog one-half inch above or below the measurements specified under "size." Size was in no way changed from the previous Standard that read: "ideal height of a dog is 19 to 22 inches; for bitches 18 to 21 inches measured across the shoulders at the highest point." The only change in height at shoulder was the substitution of one-half inch above or below to replace the word, "approximately."

As co-ownerships and one-Whippet owners become more important in American Whippet activities, membership in the AWC has stabilized at slightly over 200. Very few members allow their membership to lapse, but many owners cannot qualify under the simplest terms required to join the AWC. Every effort is made to encourage new members to join the American Whippet Club who consider their interest in the breed long-term and serious.

Mrs. Pat Dresser became editor of the *Whippet News* in 1975 after Mrs. Cormany resigned the position in 1974 due to poor health and other pressing responsibilities.

The American Whippet Club, as Parent Club for the breed, must operate for the national interest of the membership. Written surveys are conducted with the entire membership every three years to learn the needs and interests of the membership. Most of the personal and minority group conflicts that existed when the American Whippet Club slowly changed from a small Eastern organization to a truly national breed club have disappeared. Most members now think in terms of objectivity and national progress. The old feeling of, "What does the American Whippet Club do for me?" has changed to "What can I contribute to the progress of the American Whippet Club?" Since the original founding of the American Whippet Club on January 11, 1930 in Darien, Connecticut, the presidency of the Club has changed hands 10 times:

1930-34	Mr. Wyatt T. Mayer
1934	Mr. Quentin Twachtman
1935-53	Mr. Harry T. Peters, Jr.
1953-56	Mrs. Margaret Raynor
1956-59	Mr. Harry T. Peters, Jr.
1959-64	Mr. Donald Hostetter
1964-65	Mrs. Margaret Newcombe
1965-72	Mr. Victor A. Renner
1972-75	Mrs. Philip S.P. Fell
1975-76	Mr. Louis Pegram

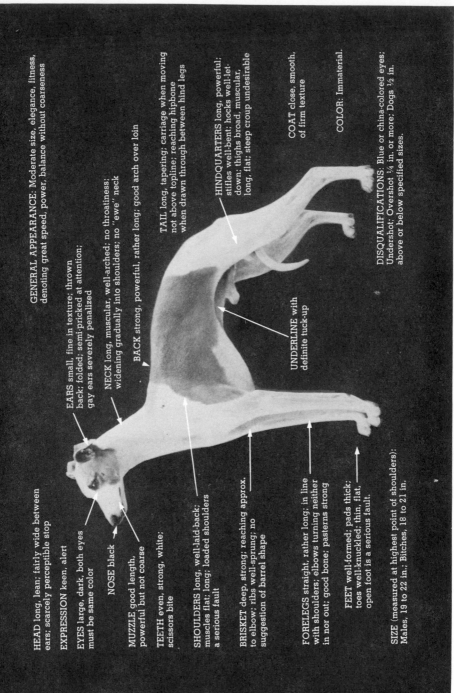

GENERAL APPEARANCE: Moderate size, elegance, fitness, denoting great speed, power, balance without coarseness

HEAD long, lean; fairly wide between ears; scarcely perceptible stop

EXPRESSION keen, alert

EYES large, dark, both eyes must be same color

NOSE black

MUZZLE good length, powerful but not coarse

TEETH even, strong, white; scissors bite

EARS small, fine in texture; thrown back; folded; semi-pricked at attention; gay ears severely penalized

NECK long, muscular, well-arched; no throatiness; widening gradually into shoulders; no "ewe" neck

BACK strong, powerful, rather long; good arch over loin

TAIL long, tapering; carriage when moving not above topline; reaching hipbone when drawn through between hind legs

SHOULDERS long, well-laid-back; muscles flat; long; loaded shoulders a serious fault

BRISKET deep, strong; reaching approx. to elbow; ribs well-sprung; no suggestion of barrel shape

UNDERLINE with definite tuck-up

HINDQUARTERS long, powerful; stifles well-bent; hocks well-let-down; thighs broad, muscular, long; flat; steep croup undesirable

FORELEGS straight, rather long; in line with shoulders; elbows turning neither in nor out; good bone; pasterns strong

FEET well-formed; pads thick; toes well-knuckled; thin, flat, open foot is a serious fault.

SIZE (measured at highest point of shoulders): Males, 19 to 22 in.; Bitches, 18 to 21 in.

COAT close, smooth, of firm texture

COLOR: Immaterial.

DISQUALIFICATIONS: Blue or china-colored eyes; Undershot; Overshot ¼ in. or more; Dogs ½ in. above or below specified sizes.

Visualization of the Whippet Standard, reprinted with permission from *Dog Standards Illustrated*, © Howell Book House 1975.

172

10

Official Standard
of the Whippet

E<small>VERY</small> breed registered by the American Kennel Club is covered by a word description of the breed. The American Kennel Club absolutely requires that each breed club have a specific word standard for their breed.

The Constitution and By-Laws of the American Whippet Club state under Section 2, Objective, Item b: *To urge members and breeders to accept the Standard of the breed as approved by the American Kennel Club as the only standard of excellence by which the Whippet shall be judged.*

Evolution of the Standard

The Whippet Standard has been changed very little since the breed was first accepted to the Stud Book of the American Kennel Club. The most radical change came—in size—between 1930 and 1944. Size was increased for dogs from 18-20" to 19-22" and for bitches from 17-19" to 18-21". The English insist on a smaller Whippet while most Americans prefer a slightly taller and more elegant individual. The height and size battle has continued to rage off and on through the years, but it has been a battle of words with few changes in height in either the American or English Standard.

During the 1960's there was real abuse of the height limits by some old-line Whippet breeders, breeder-judges and racing enthusiasts who used extreme physical advantages to win races. Some of these owners were directly connected with border-line Greyhound racing and coursing on a small scale. When one generation of race Whippets suddenly increases in height, length and weight, it became increasingly clear the Whippet Standard needed change to control the rapidly-growing height and size of some Whippets in America. On October 12, 1971 the American Kennel Club approved the recommendation of the majority of the American Whippet Club to remove from the Standard the word, APPROXIMATE, replacing it with DISQUALIFICATION reading: Size - Ideal height for dogs, 19-22 inches; for bitches, 18-21 inches measured across the shoulders at the highest point. One-half inch above or below the above stated measurements will disqualify.

The Board of Directors immediately voted that disqualifications covered in the Whippet Standard should also apply to Official Rules and Regulations for National Whippet Racing. Less than two percent of Whippets in the show ring or racing were affected by the size disqualification, but the bitterness of a few individuals seeking personal gain and prestige created virtually an armed conflict in all phases of American Whippet Club activities.

It has been said that one picture is worth a thousand words. This chapter includes the various Standards of the past 45 years and diagrams showing Whippet faults and virtues. While most knowledgeable owners, breeders and judges easily recognize the Whippet as a Whippet from reading the Standard or reviewing outstanding pictures or actual personal contact with dogs there is still much division in thinking regarding the "ideal type." There is equally as much division in interpretation on how conformation faults should be compared when judging in the ring. Certainly, a Standard for the breed is of obvious importance. But, at best the Standard must be considered a word guide, backed up by the opinion of the person evaluating an individual dog's conformation based on personal interpretation.

Standard Of The Breed
1930

Head: Long and lean, fairly wide between the ears, scarcely perceptible stop, good length of muzzle, which should be powerful without being coarse.

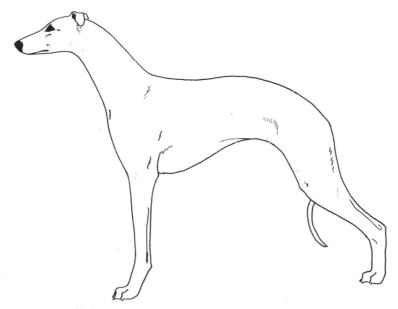

General appearance: A moderate-size sight hound giving the appearance of elegance and fitness, denoting great speed, power and balance without coarseness. A true sporting hound that covers a maximum of distance with a minimum of lost motion.

Gait

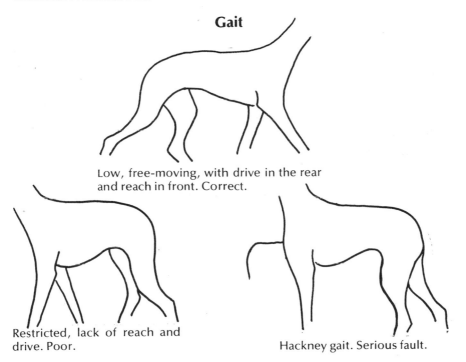

Low, free-moving, with drive in the rear and reach in front. Correct.

Restricted, lack of reach and drive. Poor.

Hackney gait. Serious fault.

Ears: Small, fine in texture, thrown back and folded. Semi-pricked when at attention. Gay ears incorrect.

Eyes: Bright, intelligent and dark.

Teeth: White, strong and even. Upper jaw should fit nicely over lower.

Neck: Long and muscular, well arched with no suggestion of throatiness, widening gradually into shoulders.

Shoulders: Oblique and muscular, without being loaded.

Chest: Deep and capacious, as wide as consistent with speed. Ribs fairly well sprung.

Forelegs: Straight and rather long, held in line with shoulders. Elbows neither in nor out, moving freely with point of shoulder. Pasterns strong. Fair amount of bone.

Feet: Either cat or hare foot is permissible. Must be well formed, with strong pads and claws, well knuckled up.

Hindquarters: Long and powerful, stifles well bent, thighs broad and muscular, hocks well let down.

Back: Broad and square, rather long and well arched over the loin, which should be strong and powerful

Tail: Long and tapering.

Coat: Close, smooth and firm in texture

Color: Immaterial.

Height: Dogs from 18 to 20 inches. Bitches from 17 to 19 inches.

Standard Of The Breed - 1944

Head: Long and lean, fairly wide between the ears, scarcely perceptible stop, good length of muzzle, which should be powerful without being coarse. Nose entirely black.

Ears: Small, fine in texture, thrown back and folded. Semipricked when at attention. Gay ears are incorrect and should be severely penalized.

Eyes: Bright, intelligent, round in shape and dark hazel in color. Light yellow or oblique eyes should be strictly penalized.

Teeth: White, strong and even. Teeth of upper jaw should fit closely over the lower.

Neck: Long and muscular, well arched with no suggestion of throatiness, widening gradually into the shoulders.

Shoulders: Well laid back and muscular without being loaded.

Brisket: Very deep and strong, reaching to point of elbow. Ribs sprung but with no suggestion of barrel shape.

Forelegs: Straight and rather long, held in line with shoulders. Elbows should turn neither in nor out and move freely with the point of the shoulder. Pasterns strong. Fair amount of bone.

Feet: Must be well formed with strong, thick pads and well knuckled up claws.

Hindquarters: Long and powerful, stifles well bent, thighs broad and muscular, hocks short and well let down. A steep croup is very undesirable

Back: Strong and powerful, rather long and very well arched over the loin, creating a definite tuck-up of the underline.

Tail: Long and tapering, should reach the hip bone when drawn through between the hind legs.

Coat: Close, smooth and firm in texture.

Ideal Height: Dogs from 19-22 inches, bitches from 18-21. These are not intended to be definite limits, only approximate .

Color: Immaterial.

Disqualification: Undershot mouth.

Approved July 11, 1944

Proper Balance in the Whippet

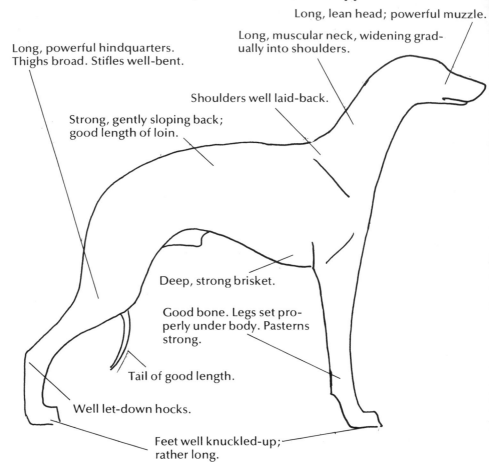

Long, lean head; powerful muzzle.

Long, muscular neck, widening gradually into shoulders.

Long, powerful hindquarters.
Thighs broad. Stifles well-bent.

Shoulders well laid-back.

Strong, gently sloping back;
good length of loin.

Deep, strong brisket.

Good bone. Legs set properly under body. Pasterns strong.

Tail of good length.

Well let-down hocks.

Feet well knuckled-up;
rather long.

Undesirable Qualities

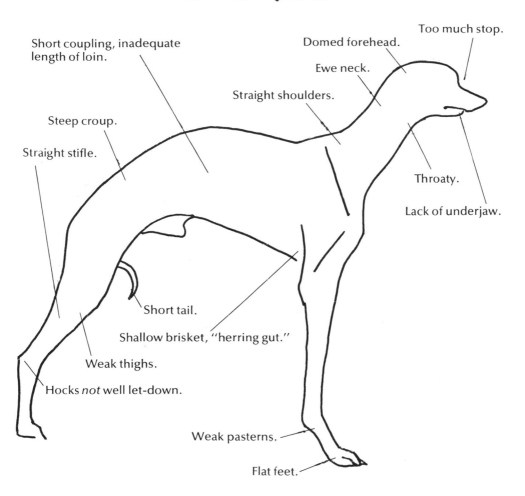

Too much stop.

Domed forehead.

Short coupling, inadequate length of loin.

Ewe neck.

Straight shoulders.

Steep croup.

Straight stifle.

Throaty.

Lack of underjaw.

Short tail.

Shallow brisket, "herring gut."

Weak thighs.

Hocks *not* well let-down.

Weak pasterns.

Flat feet.

Standard Of The Breed - 1955

General Appearance: The Whippet should be a dog of moderate size, very alert, that can cover a maximum of distance with a minimum of lost motion, a true sporting hound. Should be put down in hard condition but with no suggestion of being muscle-bound.

Head: Long and lean, fairly wide between the ears, scarcely perceptible stop, good length of muzzle which should be powerful without being coarse. Nose entirely black.

Ears: Small, fine in texture, thrown back and folded. semipricked when at attention. Gay ears are incorrect and should be severely penalized.

Eyes: Large, intelligent, round in shape and dark hazel in color, must be at least as dark as the coat color. Expression should be keen and alert. Light yellow or oblique eyes should be strictly penalized. A sulky expression and lack of alertness to be considered most undesirable

Teeth: White, strong and even. Teeth of upper jaw should fit closely over the lower. An undershot mouth shall disqualify.

Neck: Long and muscular, well-arched and with no suggestion of throatiness, widening gradually into the shoulders. Must not have any tendency to a "ewe" neck.

Shoulders: Long, well laid back with long, flat muscles. Loaded shoulders are a very serious fault.

Brisket: Very deep and strong, reaching as nearly as possible to the point of the elbow. Ribs well sprung but with no suggestion of barrel shape. Should fill in the space between the forelegs so that there is no appearance of a hollow between them.

Forelegs: Straight and rather long, held in line with the shoulders and not set under the body so as to make a forechest. Elbows should turn neither in nor out and move freely with the point of the shoulder. Fair amount of bone, which should carry right down to the foot. Pasterns strong.

Feet: Must be well formed with strong, thick pads and well-knuckled paws. A thin, flat, open foot is a serious fault.

Hindquarters: Long and powerful, stifles well bent, hocks well let down

Head & Ears

Long, lean head with little stop, fairly wide between ears. Good.

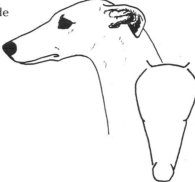

Broad head with short muzzle. Domed skull. Poor.

Lacking underjaw, overbite, narrow head. Roman nose.

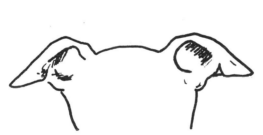

Semi-pricked. Correct.

Soft, unfolded. Faulty.

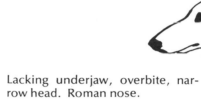

Gay or pricked. Faulty

and close to the ground. Thighs broad and muscular, the muscles should be long and flat. A steep croup is most undesirable.

Back: Strong and powerful, rather long with a good, natural arch over the loin creating a definite tuck-up of the underline but covering a lot of ground.

Tail: Long and tapering, should reach to a hipbone when drawn through between the hind legs. Must not be carried higher than the top of the back when moving.

Coat: Close, smooth and firm in texture.

Size: Ideal height for dogs, 19 to 22 inches; for bitches, 18 to 21 inches. These are not intended to be definite limits, only approximate.

Gait: Low, free moving and smooth, as long as is commensurate with the size of the dog. A short, mincing gait with high knee action should be severely penalized.

Color: Immaterial.

Disqualifications: Undershot mouth.

Approved November 9, 1955

Standard Of The Breed - 1971

General Appearance: A moderate size sight hound giving the appearance of elegance and fitness, denoting great speed, power, and balance without coarseness. A true sporting hound that covers a maximum of distance with a minimum of lost motion.

Head: Long and lean, fairly wide between the ears, scarcely perceptible stop, good length of muzzle which should be powerful without being coarse. Nose entirely black.

Ears: Small, fine in texture, thrown back and folded. Semipricked when at attention. Gay ears are incorrect and should be severely penalized

Eyes: Large, dark, with keen intelligent alert expression. Lack of pigmentation around eyelids is undesirable. Yellow or dilute-colored eyes should

182

Eyes

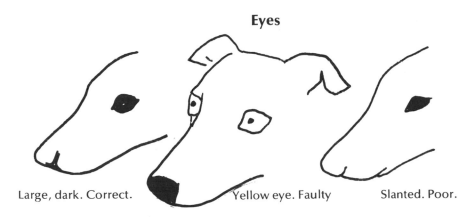

Large, dark. Correct. Yellow eye. Faulty Slanted. Poor.

Bite

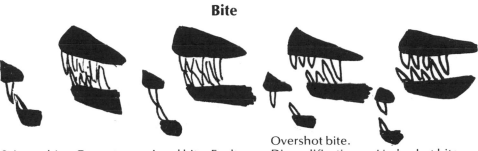

Scissors bite. Correct. Level bite. Faulty. Overshot bite. Disqualification. Undershot bite. Disqualification.

Necks

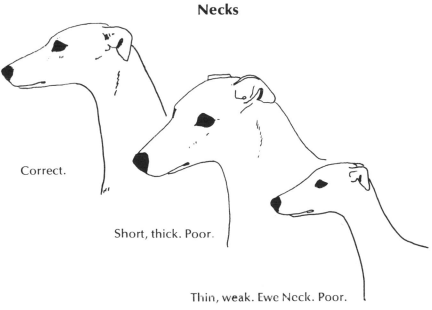

Correct.

Short, thick. Poor.

Thin, weak. Ewe Neck. Poor.

be strictly penalized. Blue or china-colored eyes shall disqualify. Both eyes must be of the same color.

Muzzle: Muzzle should be long and powerful denoting great strength of "bite" without coarseness. Teeth should be white and strong. Teeth of upper jaw should fit closely over teeth of lower jaw creating a strong scissors bite. Extremely short muzzle or lack of underjaw should be strictly penalized. An even bite is extremely undesirable. Undershot shall disqualify. Overshot one-quarter inch or more shall disqualify.

Neck: Long and muscular, well-arched and with no suggestion of throatiness, widening gradually into the shoulders. Must not have any tendency to a "ewe" neck.

Shoulders: Long, well-laid back with long, flat muscles. Loaded shoulders are a *very* serious fault.

Brisket: Very deep and strong, reaching as nearly as possible to the point of the elbow. Ribs well sprung but with no suggestion of barrel shape. Should fill in the space between the forelegs so that there is no appearance of a hollow between them.

Forelegs: Straight and rather long, held in line with the shoulders and *not* set under the body so as to make a forechest. Elbows should turn neither in nor out and move freely with the point of the shoulder. Fair amount of bone, which should carry right down to the feet. Pasterns strong.

Feet: Must be well formed with strong, thick pads and well-knuckled-up paws. A thin, flat, open foot is a serious fault.

Hindquarters: Long and powerful, stifles well bent, hocks well let down and close to the ground. Thighs broad and muscular, the muscles should be long and flat. A steep croup is most undesirable.

Back: Strong and powerful, rather long with a good, natural arch over the loin creating a definite tuck-up of the underline but covering a lot of ground.

Tail: Long and tapering, should reach to a hipbone when drawn through between the hind legs. Must not be carried higher than the top of the back when moving.

Coat: Close, smooth, and firm in texture.

Fronts

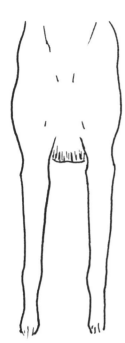

Straight front legs. Good width and depth of brisket. Correct.

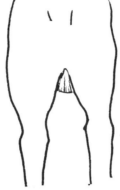

Shallow brisket with hollow between front legs. Faulty.

Barrel ribs. Faulty.

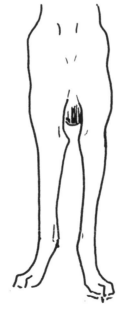

Narrow front. Tied-in elbows, Toeing out. Faulty.

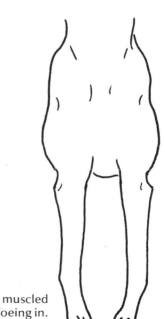

Heavily muscled shoulder. Toeing in. Faulty.

185

Color: Immaterial.

Size: Ideal height for dogs, 19 to 22 inches; for bitches, 18 to 21 inches, measured across the shoulders at the highest point. One-half inch above or below the above stated measurements will disqualify.

Gait: Low, free moving and smooth, as long as is commensurate with the size of the dog. A short, mincing gait with high knee action should be severely penalized.

Disqualifications: Blue or china-colored eyes. Undershot. Overshot one-quarter inch or more. A dog one-half inch above or below the measurements specified under "Size".

Approved October 12, 1971

The Current Whippet Standard

General Appearance: A moderate size sight hound giving the appearance of elegance and fitness, denoting great speed, power, and balance without coarseness. A true sporting hound that covers a maximum of distance with a minimum of lost motion.

Head: Long and lean, fairly wide between the ears, scarcely perceptible stop, good length of muzzle which should be powerful without being coarse. Nose entirely black.

Ears: Small, fine in texture, thrown back and folded. Semipricked when at attention. Gay ears are incorrect and should be severely penalized.

Eyes: Large, dark, with keen intelligent alert expression. Lack of pigmentation around eyelids is undesirable. Yellow or dilute-colored eyes should be strictly penalized. Blue or china-colored eyes shall disqualify. Both eyes must be of the same color.

Muzzle: Muzzle should be long and powerful denoting great strength of "bite" without coarseness. Teeth should be white and strong. Teeth of upper jaw should fit closely over teeth of lower jaw creating a strong scissors bite. Extremely short muzzle or lack of underjaw should be strictly penalized. An even bite is extremely undesirable. Undershot shall disqualify. Overshot one-quarter inch or more shall disqualify.

Neck: Long, clean and muscular, well arched with no suggestion of

Pasterns

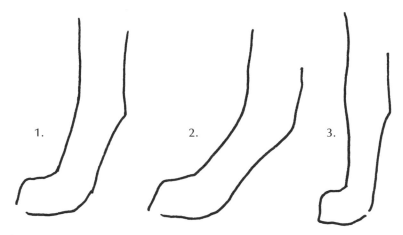

1. Well-bent. Correct.
Faulty.

2. Weak. Faulty.

3. Straight. Knuckled over.

Toenails

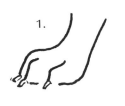

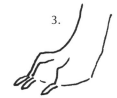

1. Proper length.

2. Too Short.

3. Too long.

Feet

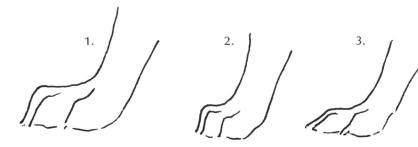

1. Hare foot. Correct

2. Cat foot. Correct.

3. Flat, splayed foot. Faulty.

throatiness, widening gracefully into the top of the shoulder. A short thick neck, or concave curvature of the top neckline sometimes called ewe (opposite of arched), should be penalized.

Shoulders: Long, well laid back, with flat muscles, allowing for moderate space between shoulder blades at the peak of withers. The length of the shoulder blade equals the length of the upper arm. A straight shoulder blade, short upper arm, a heavily muscled or loaded shoulder, or a very narrow shoulder, all restricting low free movement, should be strictly penalized.

Brisket: Very deep and strong, reaching as nearly as possible to the point of the elbow. Ribs well sprung but with no suggestion of barrel shape. Should fill in the space between the forelegs so that there is no appearance of a hollow between them.

Back and Loin: The back broad, firm and well muscled, having length and a strong natural arch over the loin, creating a definite tuck-up of the underline. A short loin creating a cramped stance should be penalized.

Topline and Croup: The topline runs smoothly from the withers with a graceful and not too accentuated arch beginning over the loin and carrying through over the croup, with the arch being continuous without flatness. A wheelback, flat back, dip behind shoulder blades, or a back that falls away sharply creating a cut-away appearance should be penalized. A steep or flat croup should be penalized.

Forelegs: Straight, giving appearance of strength and substance of bone. The points of the elbows should point neither in nor out, but straight back. When the dog moves, the joints allow free movement from the point of the shoulder to give a long low reach. Pasterns strong, slightly bent and flexible. Bowed legs, tied-in elbows, legs lacking substance, legs set far under the body so as to create a forechest, weak or straight pasterns should be strictly penalized.

Feet: Feet must be well formed with hard, thick pads and strong nails. Nails naturally short or of moderate length. Toes should be long, close and well arched. Feet more hare than cat, but both are acceptable. Flat, open, or soft feet without thick hard pads, should be strictly penalized.

Hindquarters: Long and powerful, stifles well bent, hocks well let down and close to the ground. Thighs broad and muscular. The muscles are long and flat and carry well down toward the hock. Sickle or cowhocks should be strictly penalized.

Shoulder, Brisket and Chest

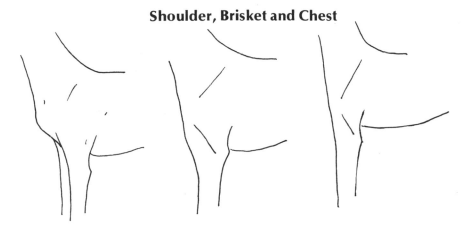

1. Legs set too far under shoulders. Shallow brisket. Faulty.   2. Legs properly set. Good brisket. Correct.   3. Legs set too far forward. Straight shoulder. Shallow brisket. Faulty.

Back, Loin, Topline and Croup Faults

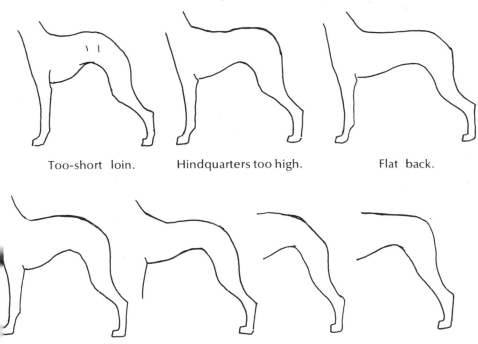

Too-short loin.   Hindquarters too high.   Flat back.

Accentuated arch.   Dip behind shoulder   Steep croup.   Flat croup.
                         blades.

Hindquarters

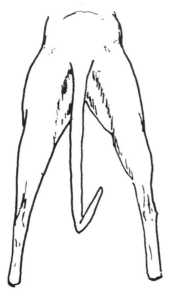

Long, powerful quarter. Muscles well down toward hock. Correct.

Weak, thin thighs. Hock not low to ground. Not enough bend of stifle. Faulty.

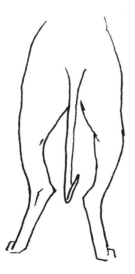

Cow hocks. Faulty.

Sickle hocks. Faulty.

Tail: The tail long and tapering, reaching to the hipbone when drawn through between the legs. When the dog is in motion, the tail is carried low with a gentle upward curve; tail should not be carried higher than top of back. A curled tail should be penalized.

Coat and Color: Close, smooth and firm in texture. A coarse, or wooly coat should be penalized. Color immaterial.

Gait: Low, free moving and smooth, with reach in the forequarters and strong drive in the hindquarters. The dog has great freedom of action when viewed from the side; the forelegs reach forward close to the ground; the hindlegs have strong propelling power. Lack of front reach or rear drive, a short, mincing gait with high knee action should be strictly penalized. When moving and viewed from front or rear, legs should turn neither in nor out, nor should feet cross or interfere with each other. Crossing in front or moving too close should be strictly penalized.

N.B.: Old scars and injuries, the result of work or accident should not be allowed to prejudice the dog's chance in the show ring, unless they interfere with its movement or ability to perform.

Size: Ideal height for dogs, 19 to 22 inches; for bitches, 18 to 21 inches, measured across the shoulders at the highest point. One-half inch above or below the above stated measurements will disqualify.

Disqualifications: Blue or china-colored eyes. Undershot. Overshot one-quarter inch or more. A dog one-half inch above or below the measurements specified under "Size."

Approved March 9, 1976

They're off! At the breakaway of a Midwest race meeting Volant's Big Red Machine (#1) takes the lead from her good position on the outside.

11

Whippet Racing as Approved by the American Whippet Club

THE VERSATILITY of the Whippet continues to amaze me. It seems virtually impossible that a placid, lovable, streamlined dog can be peacefully reclining on a couch in the home, yet when asked, can explode from a starting box, running 200 yards in from 11 to 14 seconds. No other breed so richly deserves the title "Speed and Beauty."

During my lifetime it has been difficult to establish the Whippet in America as a popular breed, especially as a pet. It is also difficult to make crystal clear that the Whippet pound for pound is the fastest breed of dog in the world. Yet, all these things he is.

The Whippet has retained his combination of beauty and speed both in the United States and England in spite of diverse opinions of owners and breeders who breed, race, and show their dogs. A few members of The American Whippet Club have desparately tried to unite Whippet owners as to the versatility of the breed, thus the formation of *Official Rules And Regulations for National Whippet Racing* and establishment of The Award of Racing Merit Program. Progress, within the limits of available Whippet population at times might be considered good, yet Whippet rac-

Grave Digger (#4, third from left), owned by the author, puts forward a maximum effort to win this race at the Mississippi Valley meeting.

Mare's Head Speed to Spare is captured by the camera with all four feet off the ground as he moves away from his field. *Mains.*

ing in North America still remains a very minor sport, held largely in California, Illinois, Ohio, Missouri, Iowa, Nevada, Washington, and British Columbia. Whippet entries at major race meetings, approved by the AWC, compare favorably in number to the largest Whippet entries at Specialty and supported entry shows. It is hard to realize there were more trained race Whippets around Baltimore, Maryland from 1935 to 1945 than there have been in this country and Canada during the past 10 years.

Many fanciers and impartial writers for the media including *the Wall Street Journal*, have been amazed that there has not been greater growth in Whippet racing as an amateur sport and a fine, family hobby. The press, like the author believes, that Whippet racing is a sleeping giant. Hopefully more owners devoted to dual purpose dogs will give the Whippet his just credit for being such a versatile athelete and a superior pet.

Many Whippet owners have made major contributions to national Whippet racing since reintroduction of the sport in the late 1950s, as a breed improvement program. Their names and their activities are mentioned in Chapters 4 and 5 of this book.

A number of clubs promote the dual purpose Whippet with emphasis on racing and publish monthly news letters. These are: *Speed*, official publication of Northern California Whippet Fanciers Assoc.; *The Rag Runner*, official publication of Southern California Whippet Assoc.; *Lead And Lure*, official publication of the Great Western Whippet Assoc.; *Tri-State Whippet Report*, official publication of Tri-State Whippet Assoc.; *Midwest Coursing News Letter*, *Whippet Paws*, official publication of Northern California Whippet Breeders Association. *Hare N' Hound*, official publication of Whippet Club of San Diego,

The author has been the National Racing Secretary for the American Whippet Club, since Whippet racing was revived in the mid-1950s. The official publication of the American Whippet Club, the *Whippet News*, reports all national race activities.

Official Rules and Regulations
for National Whippet Racing

(1975)

I. **Organization**

The President of the American Whippet Club each year selects a National Racing Secretary who must be a member in good standing of the American Whippet Club. The National Racing Secretary is responsible to the President of the American Whippet Club but need not be a member of the Board Of Directors.

The National Racing Secretary selects two members of the American Whippet

Club to assist in formulating Official Rules and Regulations for National Whippet Racing and the Award of Racing Merit Program. This group of three constitutes the National Racing Rules Committee.

The American Kennel Club does not supervise dog racing of any type. The American Whippet Club is a member of the American Kennel Club and offers Official Rules and Regulations for National Whippet Racing to its members as a breed improvement program. *The American Whippet Club, as an organization, does not operate Whippet race meetings. Authority is delegated to an individual member or group of members to properly supervise and conduct race meetings as covered in Official Rules and Regulations for National Whippet Racing. The American Whippet Club sets the policy for conduct of National Whippet Racing, but it is the ultimate responsibility of local race members or groups to enforce this policy.*

II. **Purpose**
  A. To encourage properly trained race Whippets to compete against each other under Official Rules and Regulations for National Whippet Racing. (All Whippets must be litter or individually registered with AKC or Registration Bureaus that are acceptable to the AKC in the transfer of registration papers.)

  An approved race meeting under Official Rules and Regulations for National Whippet Racing should be conducted on the same high standard as an American Whippet Club specialty show. (It should be a showcase of racing quality.)

  B. To respect the Whippet as a racer, a show dog and as a friend resulting in:
    1. Speed, endurance and intelligence to be highly competitive while racing against other Whippets.

    2. Proper conformation to be competitive in the show ring.

    3. Willing understanding to be an ideal kennel or house pet.
  C. To reward outstanding race Whippets with an Award of Racing Merit Certicate when they have accumulated the necessary Award of Racing Merit points as outlined in the Award of Racing Merit program.

Why the muzzle is important—Four dogs fighting for the lead can get very excited in a close race. Muzzling dogs is a wise and necessary precaution.

Van Oorshcott's Toro (#1) taking the lead from Zephyr, CD (#4) in a strong field of California racers.

"Poetry in motion."

THE AMERICAN WHIPPET CLUB

Award of Racing Merit Certificate

This certifies that

THE WHIPPET_____

OWNED BY_____

has accumulated the required 15 points under OFFICIAL RULES
AND REGULATIONS FOR NATIONAL WHIPPET RACING to receive
THE AWARD OF RACING MERIT CERTIFICATE.

CERTIFICATE NO._____19____

_____
President

DATE_____19____

_____
National Racing Secretary

LITHO IN U.S.A.

The Award of Racing Merit Certificate. This is presented by the American Whippet Club for dogs that qualify. The affix ARM has been proudly carried by many of the finest racing Whippets in the United States and Canada since inception of the program.

12

The Award of
Racing Merit Program

THE AWARD of Racing Merit Program (ARM) was originated to honor the top racing Whippets running under Official Rules and Regulations for National Whippet Racing as approved by the AWC. A point system (do not confuse with points used in rotating Whippets by races) requires a Whippet to earn 15 ARM points before he is eligible to secure the award and a framed certificate signed by the President of the American Whippet Club and National Racing Secretary.

Award of Racing Merit winners who have earned the necessary points continue to race in the regular adult grading system at race meetings held under Official Rules and Regulations for national Whippet racing. *They do not accumulate additional award points after they earn the 15 necessary points to win an ARM certificate.* So, a dog who has not won an ARM who finishes second in total final point standing behind an ARM winner, acturally receives the highest number of award points based on the number of adults entered in the official race meeting, including ARM winners. An ARM winner counts as an award point entry in an official race meeting but cannot accumulate additional ARM points in the race. This program is scored like the system used in the show ring. Once a show dog has become a champion, he no longer accumulates additional championship points in Best of Breed competition.

Whippet racing started in 1958 under the supervision of The American Whippet Club. It was not until 1966 that the Award of Racing Merit Certificate program was originated. Outstanding racing Whippets to win Award of Racing Merit Certificates through 1975 are:

Whippet	Award Year	Owner	State	Sex
Strathoak Spring Intrigue	1967	Pegram	Missouri	M
Titan Hobo	1968	Raczak	Illinois	M
Bardon Sara Lawrence	1968	Trounce	California	M
Ch. Pinetops				
Opening Knight	1968	Hammond	California	M
Ch. Marial's Jellybean, C.D.	1969	Strauss-Arthur	Wisconsin	M
Caesar	1969	Varga	Illinois	M
Emberson Of Course	1969	Fraser	B.C.	M
Can. Ch. Rock-a-Bye				
Ember Of Course	1969	Turpin, Jr.	B.C.	F
Scram Whisper	1970	Klintworth	Wisconsin	F
Scram I'm First	1970	Blackstone-	Wisconsin	F
		Fischer		
Fortuna Fair Annet	1970	Robinson	New York	F
Renfield Lady O'Lazebrook	1970	Murray-Gutilla	Ohio	F
Whirlaway's Magnificent				
Lance	1970	Grim	California	M
Brenda's Champagne	1970	Clift	Ohio	M
Ch. Whirlaway's Apache, C.D.	1971	Hayhurst	California	M
Riverdale's Charmaine	1971	Purvis	Ohio	F
Ralson Gingerbread Boy	1971	Kinch	Illinois	M
Brenda's Brandy	1971	Clift	Ohio	M
Change In Destiny	1971	Pegram	Missouri	M
Epinard's Shelby				
Of Wyndsor	1971	Balint	California	M
Marial's Chancellor	1971	Strauss-Arthur	Wisconsin	M
Heathcliffe Basha	1972	Yasunga	California	M
Can. Ch. Epinard's Sonny				
Jim Of Course	1972	Turpin, Sr.	B. C.	M
Destructor	1972	Tolley	Missouri	M
Volant Fat Albert	1972	Helton	Ohio	M
He Ain't Country	1972	Mauillo	Missouri	M
Uruhu's Karma	1972	Bangs	Missouri	F
Madcap Midnight Cowboy	1972	Rosenstock-	California	M
		Valenti		
Legendary Knight Bright	1972	Carlson	California	F
Antonio's Quick Silver	1973	Mauillo	Missouri	M
Can. Ch. Renfield				
Temptress Of Course	1973	Rankin	B. C.	F
Ch. Marial's Traymatt				
Snowman	1973	Strauss-Arthur	Wisconsin	M
Featherstone's				
Mr. Lightfoot	1973	Steckel	California	M
Van Oorschot's Toro	1973	Marten	California	M
Uruhu's Flying Fantasy	1973	Theiss	Missouri	F
Marial's Renfield				
Phalarope	1973	Strauss-Arthur	Wisconsin	M
Cricket Hearth				
Chief Joseph	1973	Pruett-Weaver	Ohio	M

Strathoak Spring Intrigue (Strathoak Will-O-The-Wisp ex Strathoak Summer Breeze), owned by the author and bred by Christine Cormany, was the first dog to earn the Award of Racing Merit.

Epinard's Shelby of Wyndsor, ARM (Can. Ch. Emberson of Course ex Eyleland Hannah), owned by Jean Balint, established a nationwide record as one of the finest race Whippets of all time.

Volant's Big Red Machine, ARM, shown with owners Donna Helton (left) and Mary K. Gluhm, was the top racer in the Midwest for 1974 and 1975

Oh Golly Ms. Molly, ARM, owned by Jeanne Thomas.

Legendary Knight Bright, ARM, owned by Bud Carlson

Ch. Pinetop's Opening Knight, ARM, owned by Donna Valenti was one of the dogs that dominated the racing scene during the time he was competing. His lasting contribution though was as a sire. Seven of his get have the ARM title, and at this writing he is the sire of 14 champions.

Van Oorschot's Toro, ARM, owned by Denna Marten, has an outstanding track record. Along with many previous victories, he was unbeaten on the track during 1975.

Topper's Oh Golly Miss Molly	1973	Thomas	California	F
Crick-E-Su's Alamatheus, C.D.	1973	Horton	California	F
Volant's Big Red Machine	1973	Gluhm	Ohio	F
Topper's Joe Willy Machine	1974	Hammond-Valenti	California	M
Volant's Buckeye Express	1974	Helton	Ohio	M
Limited Edition O'Lazebrook	1974	Strauss-Arthur	Wisconsin	M
Featherstone's First Edition	1974	Smith	Illinois	M
Big Star Jet	1974	Hickmon	California	M
Regalstock Lord Weasel O'Topper	1974	Mathewson	California	M
Power Of Destiny	1974	Pegram	Missouri	M
Wynrick's High Intensity	1975	Rickard	California	M
Knight-Kap O'Lazebrook	1975	Henry-Gutilla	Ohio	M
Topper's T.N.T.	1975	Van Oorschot	California	M
Coventry's Golden Poppy	1975	Burt-Barlow	California	F
Bayview Day Bright	1975	Carlson	California	F

The Award of Merit Point Schedule is as Follows

50 Adult Whippets or More

Based on starters not entries:

6 points - High Point Winner
4 points - Second High Point Winner
2 points - Third High Point Winner

40 to 49 Adult Starters

5 points - High Point Winner
3 points - Second High Point Winner
1 point - Third Point Winner

30 to 39 Adult Starters

4 points - High Point Winner
2 points - Second High Point Winner

20 to 29 Adult Starters

3 points - High Point Winner
1 point - Second High Point Winner

These points are for flat racing only.

13

Training the
Race Whippet

THE WHIPPET registered by the American Kennel Club and the track Greyhound registered by the National Greyhound Association are the two major breeds who run with very high bursts of explosive speed. These breeds have the inherited desire to chase a moving object (lure) or course and kill game. This high speed and inherited hunting instinct in no way interfere with the ability of these dogs to be docile, loving pets. It is almost unheard of for either of these breeds to bite a person. Truly the Whippet and Greyhound are hunting dogs and must not be considered aggressive to humans.

Your First Racer

Racing Whippets can live in any normal home, and should be treated as pets and family companions. Your first race Whippet might be an untrained adult, but starting with a six- or eight-month-old puppy is preferable. Regardless of age, you follow much the same pattern of training by interesting your Whippet in chasing a moving object. Fur, imitation hair, wigs, falls and coarse pieces of cloth have great appeal. Generally, fur tied to cloth is much more appealing than a plain rag or towel. Whippets relate fur to their natural prey, and most outstanding racers hit and stay on the lure at the finish of a race. Their intent is to kill the moving object, proving fur or hair makes the superior lure. A squeaky rubber toy or rubber duck call added to the fur and cloth lure adds to the Whippet's zest for the chase. Many race Whippets have never killed a small animal of any type, yet they definitely connect a moving, noise-making fur or hair object to a live rabbit or squirrel.

Early Lure Training

Start teaching Whippet pups at about eight weeks to chase a piece of cloth tied to a six-foot rope. Drag the cloth in front of the young puppies, and they quickly learn to chase the moving object. Some will grab at the cloth, attempt to tear it up or hang on with great determination. Early lure training sessions for very young puppies should only last a few minutes at a time, not more than ten minutes every other day. Within a few days the puppies will consider this chasing and teasing with the rag great fun. As the puppies grow older, swing the cloth around your body in circles, usually tying the lure to a pole three or four feet long. Try to keep the pups from catching the rag lure quickly. Teach them to be competitive, encourage the desire to catch and kill the moving object. A man's sock with a rubber squeaky toy makes an ideal lure for very young puppies.

In most cases your first race Whippet will not have had early lure training at home. He may even shy from fox tail or fur/skin lure attached to a rag the first time it is waved in front of him. You must interest him in mouthing the lure and eventually chasing it enthusiastically. There are a number of ways this can be accomplished. First, make a lure with a six-foot piece of clothes line and cloth or fur. Attach a squeaky toy so it is more attractive to the dog. The sooner he will mouth the object, the better. If you can attract his attention with the lure on a rope, indoors or out, try to get him interested in playing with or "killing" the lure. Some owners get excellent results by placing the dog in a crate and dragging the lure outside to excite the dog. Regardless of how you get interest, the important thing is getting the dog to chase the lure in an attempt to "destroy" it. Once a Whippet has developed the desire to pursue a lure, you will have overcome the major bar to having a successful racer.

Developing a Runner

Most Whippet owners do not live near organized Whippet racing and schooling. However, this should not discourage your racing activities. When possible, take your Whippet where he can be run off leash and get the feeling of freedom. If he can see a rabbit or squirrel, he will, hopefully, give chase. Develop in your dog a feeling of freedom and hunting instinct. Lure racing should come rapidly and easily after this.

Teaching Whippets to run straight and true is most important. Have one person hold the dog while a second person, generally the owner, runs in a straight line away from the person holding the dog. While the owner is running away, he should constantly call the dog by name encouraging him to run when he is released. Start at about fifty yards and gradually increase the distance to 200 yards, but allow several weeks in spreading this distance. A couple of runs each training period, three times a week, is enough. Make these sprints fun, rewarding the Whippet with praise and encouragement when he responds well. Never run two Whippets together without a lure, as they will start to bump and play. This constitutes a foul and disqualification in regular lure racing. When the dog learns to run enthusiastically from one person to another, and will mouth or destroy the fur-cloth lure, he will probably adapt quickly when placed in competition with other Whippets in regular drag lure, straight races.

Equipment

Eventually, if you continue in Whippet racing, you will need a power-driven lure. This costs approximately $100.00. Starting boxes in most cases can be built locally at a cost of from $100.00 to $300.00 for a six-stall starting box.

All Whippets must race in comfortable muzzles. They are miniatures of Greyhound muzzles and cost about $10.00 each. When several people in an area become interested in Whippet racing, the cost of any one individual in purchasing required equipment is greatly reduced. You can find out where to get the right equipment through the AWC. The name and address of the Secretary appears in *Purebred Dogs—American Kennel Gazette*.

You will need people to operate schooling races, and the more racing Whippets available for schooling and racing, the better. All Whippets cannot be raced against each other because of differences in speed between individuals, training experience, racing habits, age, and other factors. Whippet racing is fun, but it is an exacting, competitive sport.

Learning From Other Dogs

When you begin training with a power-electric lure or a hand-wound lure, have your Whippet observe the speed of the drag lure from his crate. Place the crate near the course of the lure, but if other Whippets are

Standard racing muzzles can vary in material and design to a certain extent. All muzzles shown here can be worn by dogs running in AWC-approved race meetings.

Standard racing blankets are officially color keyed to the number: 1-red; 2-blue; 3-white; 4-green; 5-black; 6-bright yellow.

The electric lure used at major race meetings. The top had been lifted back to show the inner workings.

The first hand-wound lure used after the 1940s. It was developed by the author and other racing enthusiasts. Pads were added by Eugene Jacobs to better protect dogs at the end of a race.

schooling, don't interfere with them. Let your pupil watch other experienced racers chase and catch the lure at the finish line. This will often arouse an immediate desire to chase the lure, especially when a Whippet has been trained at home. When the dog shows enthusiasm as the lure passes his crate, he is ready to hand school after the lure. Should he go to sleep or turn his back on the lure, chances are he will not run the lure the first time. Some Whippets take quickly to chasing the lure, while others often have to observe for much longer periods of time. Generally, lack of early race training at home has a greater bearing on slow learners than the lack of hereditary desire to chase a moving object.

Schooling

The owner should not hold his own dog for schooling on the lure in early training. Rather, he should stand to the finish where the lure will come to a halt. The owner should run in a straight line from the person holding his dog to the finish line and should remain past the finish line during the first schoolings. Whether the dog chases the lure or just runs in a straight line to the owner at the finish line, he merits praise. Pick up your dog quickly at the end of his training race if he does not try to catch and mouth the lure. If he stops at the lure, then let him play with it. Show your pleasure in his fine performance by teasing him with and shaking the lure. Many confused, inexperienced racers will be attracted by other Whippets and will run off the track before the finish line, so try to school him when no other dogs are near.

The lure operator should keep the lure just in front of the inexperienced racer in early training. Some lure operators prefer to have the lure in back of the hand slipper at the start of a schooling race. Others put the lure just in front of the new race pupil. The dog should be allowed to see the lure as it starts in motion. A hand-wound lure is often better in training green racers than the power lure. The power lure moves off very quickly and can be gone before an inexperienced dog sees it. Lure operators should always keep the lure just ahead of the dog, and tease him with a jerking lure motion during the running of the schooling race. When a dog is just running to his owner standing at the finish, not trying to chase the lure, it should be kept well ahead of the dog at all times until it passes the finish line. This is all new to the pupil. Some dogs watch the lure, but are really thinking of their owners at the finish line. Experienced lure operators are vital in properly breaking new dogs to the lure. A good lure operator understands the needs of the green racer and can often create interest by teasing the dog with a short, close-up lure.

Many who own larger numbers of race Whippets will use an older, slow, experienced dog to set the example for a young dog breaking into

209

racing. Both are hand slipped by a stranger. The older dog takes the lead and is followed to the finish line by the pupil. This teaches the youngster what is expected. Never use an older dog that is too fast, too slow, or one that will fight the pupil off the lure at the finish. Never race two inexperienced dogs together until they are properly running the lure. Many fighters and bumpers are developed when young, inexperienced Whippets bump and play. They do not clearly understand that they are to chase the moving lure. Honesty on the lure at all times during the running of a race should be the prime objective of any good race Whippet.

Don't be too disappointed if your dog does not take quickly to chasing the lure, but don't be overjoyed if response is immediate. Don't overtrain on any one day. If your dog schools well, three schoolings a day are enough. If the dog does not run up-track following the lure, or to the owner at the finish line, don't continue schooling further that day after two attempts. Once a dog is properly running the lure, when possible, school alone at least once before racing him in training races with other Whippets of approximately the same speed.

A combination of desire to be first on the lure and to surpass other dogs without intentional interference generally makes for a superior racer. The better runners seem to improve after each daily schooling. Slower or disinterested animals usually level off in speed, desire and inconsistency. As a rule, inexperienced Whippets don't school more than three times on any one day. Allow, when possible, a couple of days between practice schoolings. Be sure your dog runs the lure well alone before matching with dogs of the same approximate speed. Don't run your dog with known bumpers, fighters or inexperienced racers who will fight for the lure after reaching the finish line. When your dog is fully trained on the lure, have other experienced owners pick him up at the end of a race. Many dogs become man-shy at the finish and refuse to ''kill'' the lure unless their owners are present. Allow the dog to drink small amounts of water when cooling out after a race. Allow from five to 15 minutes for cooling out, depending upon weather and fitness of your racer. Do not feed for at least 12 hours before schooling or racing.

The Starting Box

It is most important that a dog is properly schooled out of the starting box. A racer who can quickly assume the lead out of the starting box has a tremendous advantage over slow-starters. A dog leaving the starting box first has no body interference from other racers. Most track records are set when the winner has little or no body contact with other contestants.

Once the dog is reliably chasing the lure after being hand slipped, he should be introduced to the starting box. There are various ideas on box

The modern six-stall starting box showing how the one piece front door is opened.

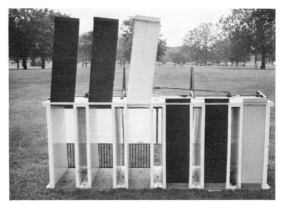

Rear view of a starting box showing three compartments open and three shut.

Dogs in the starting box ready to be off and running.

breaking, but the following method has worked best for the author. Walk your Whippet around the starting box when it is not in use. Have someone hold the dog on leash about 20 feet from the front of the box. Open the front door of the box several times to accustom the dog to the noise and motion of the flip-up door. After this, allow your dog to smell the box and get the feeling that it will not hurt him. All starting boxes have slide-up doors in the rear for each stall, or compartment, in a six-dog box. Remove the rear door of one stall, prop up the front door so it is open wide and high enough so the dog will not hit his back when leaving the box. Have someone place the dog head-first in the opening of the rear stall. Now stand about 20 feet in front of the open box calling the dog. When your dog walks or runs through the starting box toward you, he quickly realizes that the way to leave the box is from the front end. After he has come out of the box several times without fear, he is ready to break with the starting box door closed. Continue having the dog placed in the starting box from the rear, but now drop the rear door when he is safely inside his compartment. Stand in front of the closed front door calling and attracting the attention of the dog. Now run 20 or 30 yards straight away from the box still calling your dog. The person in back of the starting box should spring the catch that opens the front door. Your dog should then run straight to you. After a few successful dashes from the box, the dog is ready to break from the box, chasing the lure the full distance of the track. Again, the dog is placed in the starting box head first using the rear door. You stand in front of the box shaking the lure to keep the dog from turning around and facing the rear door. Place the lure about three feet in front of the starting box directly in front of your dog's stall, and run up-track past the finish line. The lure is started, the starting box door is opened and the dog should be ready to chase the lure the full distance of the track. Repeat once more, and if the dog responds properly, call it a day. Follow this procedure several times, allowing a few days in between each training session.

Your Whippet is now ready to compete with other dogs out of the starting box. School him the first time with a competitor he cannot outrun. Next school him with a dog he can outrun. This gives the pupil the feeling of defeat and victory, which will be a normal part of his racing life. Never school with dogs who play, fight, bump or with seasoned veterans who will fight the trainee off the lure at the finish of a race. Often when you have a large number of Whippets or Greyhounds to box-break at one time the tendency is to short cut. I often put Whippets that are schooling well after being hand slipped in the starting box with experienced racers. In most cases they will break behind the experienced racers, but quickly learn to compete. This box-breaking program saves time, and many of my young dogs do well with it. This is especially true of those who respond quickly to chasing the lure. Some Whippets broken by this method will stand backward in the starting box rather than out the opening in the starting box door. When this occurs, leave your dog in the box. He will generally right himself in the box and follow the experienced racers up the track. Most dogs soon learn to correct this habit, unaided.

Do not over box-school your dog. Once he learns to break straight and run true he will establish his own pattern of box breaking and running style in a race. Some will break fast, some slow, some will run a straight course from starting box to finish line while others will bear either to the right or left, depending on whether they draw the No. 1 inside box position or the No. 6 box, called the outside post position. It is often heart-breaking to have outstanding racers establish racing patterns that virtually eliminate their chances in a race unless they draw their favorite starting positions. So far no trainer of Greyhounds or Whippets has been able to eliminate these early established racing patterns. They become lifetime racing habits of the dogs. Sometimes a racer will change his style, but this is rare. When a racer outclasses his opponents in speed and ability, he generally does not follow his set pattern of running. There is no necessity for maneuvering when you are well ahead of the field and an easy winner. In official races, the lure is placed five or six feet in front of the starting box. This is done so all contestants can have a clear view of the lure from the box before the race begins.

Muzzle Breaking

All Whippets race in comfortable replicas of Greyhound track muzzles made of leather or plastic. This muzzle allows the dog to breathe normally and open its mouth during a race. Until a dog chases and takes hold of the lure with determination, I do not usually race him with a muzzle on. Once he attacks the lure at the finish, he then wears a properly-fitted race muzzle to avoid biting other Whippets during the battle for the lure at the finish of a race. If you have several dogs, you will need several sizes of standard racing muzzles for them.

It is important that the dog is not conscious of the muzzle during a race. Once your dog learns to fight, scratch or claw his muzzle off, you have a real problem. This difficult habit comes from the lack of proper muzzle training. Some Whippets are easier to muzzle-break than others. My program for muzzle-breaking follows. It applies well to all green racers and has worked well for me.

When your dog is six months old or more, start to muzzle-break at home before going to training at the track. Muzzle training should start with the dog on leash. Strap the muzzle on firmly or muzzle strap inside of collar so it will not slip over ears easily when the dog tries to scratch it off. Most Whippets will try to claw the muzzle off at first. On leash, the dog can be better controlled and prevented from attempting to remove his muzzle. Let him try to get the muzzle off, but be sure it stays on. Walk him on leash, discouraging his clawing and scratching. Leave the muzzle on for ten minutes the first day, and follow the same procedure every day until the pupil finally gives up. Inexperienced owners have allowed their dogs to become inveterate muzzle destroyers. Once a Whippet learns to claw off his muzzle, it becomes a great problem to correct. On several occasions I have purchased older dogs with this undesirable habit. Sometimes the habit was corrected; in others it remained a permanent problem, often greatly interfering with race performance.

Always the day before a race meet, take all the dogs to be raced for a short walk on leash with each dog's racing muzzle properly fitted. My Whippets never run muzzled off leash. The racing muzzle is used only during the running of a race. Most true muzzle fighters do the most damage to the muzzle after they are placed in the starting box. If a dog is a confirmed, spoiled muzzle fighter, use a heavier muzzle with as few seams as possible. A Whippet's claws have great destructive power and in a few seconds can destroy a good standard racing muzzle. Remember almost all muzzle fighting is from improper, early muzzle breaking at home. If the dog continues to fight his muzzle, be firm in correcting this bad habit. This is one area in which kindness will not change the habit.

Points to Remember

There is no set pattern of training that exactly fits all Whippets. Some require more exercise and training than others. All Whippets of the same size do not eat the same amount. Your success as a trainer will depend upon your ability to train each dog as an individual. Here are a few points that should assist you in keeping your dog in good racing condition:

1. Exercise the dog daily, starting at least four weeks before a race meeting. If you don't have access to enough safe, open space to let your dog run and play off leash, then walking on the leash is good. Two to five miles daily is enough. Allow your dog to run free in fields or parks at least twice a week during training. This develops wind and muscle while walking builds only strength and muscle. A Whippet who runs out of steam quickly will not race to his best advantage over the 200 yard course. Once a dog is in condition, you can cut down on the number of walks per week but always allow galloping or running exercise at least twice a week to keep the dog keen.

2. Do not feed just before a race. Allow at least 12 hours before the race. A 50–50 mixture of a good, commerical dry dog food and canned, all-meat product serves most dogs well. Allow the dry dog food to soak in water

Measuring has become an important part of Whippet race meetings. Dogs exceeding height limits or possessing other disqualifications mentioned in the Standard are barred from racing. A health check is is also conducted at this time, but the entire check takes only about 90 seconds.

Bob Theiss, the official in charge, measures Donna Helton's Volant's Fat Albert.

Whippet racing has been gaining favor since its revival in the 1950s. The training involved is more than justified by the satisfaction its followers derive.

215

Ch. Whirlaway's Apache, shown with owner Carol Hayhurst, is living proof of the Whippet's versatility. In addition to being titled in conformation he is a CD, ARM and a Pacific Coast Coursing Champion.   *Ludwig*.

for at least 15 minutes before feeding. Excessive water intake up to eight hours before a race program starts should be discouraged.

3. When you arrive at the race track, always walk your dog for a short distance and be sure he relieves himself completely before the race. Walking also relaxes the dog and takes away any stiffness that might have developed from travel.

4. After each race, walk your dog until he stops panting. This takes from five to 15 minutes, depending upon his condition and the weather. During cooling-out walks allow the dog a few laps of water at intervals, but do not allow heavy drinking at any one time. This helps cool off a racer and cuts down on dehydration. Always give the dog an opportunity to relieve himself before being returned to his crate.

5. Check toes, pads and toenails after each race. Quick attention to minor injuries is most important.

6. Keep your dog in a comfortable crate away from sight and sound of other racers. Pick a cool spot in summer and a warm spot in winter. Let your dog relax as much as possible between races.

7. Allow the dog to relieve himself again before you start for home after the race meeting has ended. A tired, comfortable, relaxed Whippet will enjoy the ride. There is also less chance of soreness and stiffness the day following a strenuous race session if he is comfortable before heading home.

Ch. Mojo's Bold Benare of Remlap, UD, owned by Ann Palmer, a winner in the conformation ring and an outstanding performer in obedience competition.

14

Obedience Training
and the Whippet

OBEDIENCE as it relates to Whippets has many meanings to the owner depending on his interest. Some owners just wish to have a dog come when called, some like to teach the dog to respond to certain commands, making him a better house pet, while others wish a Whippet for specialized obedience work and competition in AKC obedience trials. Regardless of your interest in obedience, the main purpose is better communications, trust and understanding between you and your Whippets.

Whippets as a breed, can be happy, carefree individuals, or they can be more aloof. The latter can quickly become spoiled, self-centered and other than with their owners, non-social individuals. It is often difficult to determine in advance which dogs will be best in specialized obedience work until they have started formal training. Some Whippets and Greyhounds are shy and often man shy. The is especially true of kennel-reared dogs who inherit the trait of shyness, and do not have constant, personal attention. Regardless of a Whippet's disposition, most improve in temperament when given limited, specialized obedience training. It is entirely possible that some outstanding show and race Whippets become too conscious of commands if overtrained in obedience work. There is a very delicate balance of communication between owner and dog when a Whippet is outstanding in obedience, in the show ring or on the race track. Most puppies up to six months of age, regardless of the breed, have great enthusiasm and energy, often doing many things that irritate their owners. After all, this same enthusiasm is true of young children until they start school. Don't expect great miracles of your young Whippets until they are six or more months of age. Proper leash breaking and enjoying a walk on the leash is a must with young Whippets. Teaching good manners so he enjoys people, and people in turn love and admire a dog, is most important.

Here are possible sources of training information. (1) Yellow Pages of your phone book. (2) The American Kennel Club, 51 Madison Avenue, New York City, 10010 has a special department dealing with obedience training. (3) Night adult education classes offered on dog training in many cities. (4) Purebred dog clubs in your area often sponsor obedience classes. (5) The National 4-H has a dog care training program sponsored by the Ralston Purina Company. Your County Agent should be contacted if you wish your dog to be trained under the 4-H program.

15

Training and Handling
for the Show Ring

A WHIPPET will have little chance of winning consistently in major show ring competition unless he performs in a virtually faultless manner. In most cases a slightly inferior Whippet well trained and properly handled, will win over a superior specimen that is improperly trained, or lacks enthusiasm in the show ring. Today, the show ring is filled with superior handlers both amateur and professional. Even the best handler can do little with a Whippet who does not perform properly when moving, or resists being posed for inspection by the judge. When Whippet and handler can catch the judge's eye and both are at their best in the ring, their chances of winning are excellent.

Training for the show ring starts at home. A Whippet who is properly leash-broken and lives in the house generally takes to show ring routine quickly. Kennel dogs take considerably more work, grooming and patience. There are various opinions on training for the show ring, but few will disagree that until your Whippet performs well, at home, no improvement is likely when he enters actual competition. Every Whippet is a bit different in temperament and conformation, so learn at home the faults and good points of your own dog. The secret of good handling is simply to anticipate the Whippet's action at all times, bringing out the good points and disguising or hiding the faults. A good dog and good handler who complement each other's movements, generally make a winning team.

The Best of Breed class at the 1970 Westminster Kennel Club show. When dogs of this quality meet in competition, hairline factors often make the difference between defeat and victory. This group includes some of the top dogs in the breed at that time from every section of the country. Mrs. Philip S. P. Fell was the judge (far end of ring), and selected Ch. Home Place Shandygaff (arrow), owned by Jeanne C. Henderson and handled by Robert McManus for BB. *Gilbert.*

Training for the show ring with normal Whippets should be a combination of fun and training routine. Most dogs enjoy walking on a leash, so when possible, vary your training locations to give variety. Be sure that your Whippet is comfortable gaiting on either your right or left side. Remember, in the show ring the leash is almost always held in the left hand. Your dog should always be in front of the judge, and you, the handler, are never blocking the judge's view. Dogs are creatures of habit and may resist leading on the left if not accustomed to it. Many race Whippets are broken to lead on the right side, or are walked in groups. As a result some are very slow to accept the show ring requirement of leading on the left when gaiting.

Preliminary Preparations

Most breeders start posing their Whippet puppies on a grooming table or crate at a very early age. In most cases your Whippet will enjoy standing in a normal relaxed show position so his body is properly balanced on front and rear legs. If you will pet, stroke and groom the dog for a few minutes before you stand him in a slightly exaggerated show pose, he will usually enjoy the extra attention. Once your Whippet stands well on the table, he is ready to be posed on the ground. Some inexperienced Whippets will shy or squirm when the handler first bends over them, or tries to pose them at ground level. Be patient and kind, but insist that he respond to posing just as was the case when the table or crate was used. It is often best to walk a young or inexperienced show prospect on the leash or let him work off his pent-up energy in play before attempting serious show routines.

Some young Whippets have so much energy that they just cannot respond to serious training until they become relaxed. On the other hand, sulky, sour Whippets often work better in training when fresh, and need no early preparation for their ring training. We must remember all Whippets differ in many ways. Until you know his habits, observe your Whippet closely, so there is coordination and team work between both of you.

By now your Whippet should be posing without resistance while standing on the ground, walking on your left or right side, and not resisting an "L" turn when you switch hands so that your body is not between your dog and the imaginary judge. You are now ready to have friends go over the dog with their hands similar to inspection by a judge. If your friends show and handle any breed of dog, have them pose and gait your dog, and let another stranger act as a judge, going over the Whippet with his hands. Whippets are individualistic and quickly become one-owner, spoiled pets.

If at all possible, get him accustomed to being handled by other people familiar with dogs. It is highly possible you might not be good enough as an owner handler to compete against professionals in the ring, so please make every effort to teach your Whippet to respond well to handling and moving in the hands of capable strangers at an early age.

Grooming

Whippets living in the house or in a warm climate need very little trimming to get ready for a show. In colder climates or with limited heat in the kennel a dog will generally develop a very heavy, woolly undercoat. This coat requires constant grooming with a small saw blade or fine, wire-tooth brush that will pull the undercoat, without removing the longer, stronger guard hairs. If the coat is not constantly groomed, the soft wooly undercoat will remain until it generally sheds out in late summer. Don't be confused by this soft, wooly undercoat. If your Whippet is kept out of doors, it is nature's way of protecting him form the cold.

The first hairs to trim on a Whippet are the long, coarse whiskers above and below the muzzle, running from the base of the nose above and below the mouth. The same type of whiskers can be found above the eyes and at the base of the jaw. Any type of straight scissors can be used to snip these off. Be sure to cut whiskers close to the skin. There is little chance of injury to the Whippet if you use dull-pointed straight scissors. The next area is the ears. You will find soft hairs around each ear opening. Trim out these soft hairs, and also any very soft hairs around the base of the ear. Now blend this trimming into the coat. You will note a hairline, or cowlick, running from the base of each ear down the side of the neckline. Taper these cowlicks with straight scissors so they blend smoothly with the rest of the neck. If your dog has a very heavy undercoat, remove hair from under the neck. A fine stripping knife or electric or hand clippers can be used to give length and the appearance of elegance to the neck. If the dog is not kept in a heated house and has a long coat, trim at least four weeks in advance of the show. Then even up the trimmed area with scissors or clippers the day before the show. You now move on to the area under the loin. You will find a thin line of skin between the front of the hind leg and the rib cage under the tuck-up. Level off hairline here, and trim any unsightly hair in the area under the tuck-up. This especially applies to male dogs. Move to the muscular area of hind legs and remove or even up the hairline along the rear portion of both flanks. This hairline is often called chaps or pants. Now to the tail. With a pair of straight scissors or clippers, remove all hair at the bottom of the tail running from the tip of the tail to its very base. Then cut the long hair along both sides of the tail. *Do not trim hair from top of tail.* By removing the coarse hair

The judge's resposibility is to find the best dogs in the ring and to make the appropriate awards to those most closely approaching his interpretation of the breed Standard. The exhibitor's job is to present his dog to point out its virtues and mitigate its shortcomings to the greatest possible extent.

Many official AWC race meetings feature fun matches on the program. These afford an excellent opportunity to school a young show prospect for the competition he will face in the future. Here are a group of winners at the Tri-State Whippet Club in Ohio. They are (from left) Doulas Arthur, Rich Briscoe and Laura Eyles.   *Mains.*

from the bottom of the tail and on either side, you will have a long, gracefully tapering tail.

Always respect the judge and your Whippet by showing a clean, well-groomed dog. There are many good shampoos for dogs, so select one that makes a good lather and rinse thoroughly before drying with a coarse towel. Most show Whippets are liberally marked with white. If the white areas have a yellow tinge, then a blue rinse can be used to make a clearer white. In most cases, however, a good shampoo will do the entire job. It is always well to wash at least 24 hours before showing. The coat must be given plenty of time to dry. Massage skin with hands and groom with rough towel after the coat is thoroughly dry so that the coat has a rich luster and lies flat to the skin. The short coat of the house Whippet has the advantage over the Whippet kenneled without heat. Always quickly re-groom and clean your dog just before he is ready to go in the ring.

Toenails should always be trimmed to the quick. Use a guillotine type nail cutter, Trim at least two days before showing just in case you should sever a quick. The nails bleed very freely when the quick, or vein, is cut, but seldom is the dog sore for more than a few minutes. Use a styptic stick to stop bleeding when a toe nail is accidently cut too short. Try not to cut into the quick, but use your nail cutters as close to the quick as possible. Nails on all Whippets are not the same. Some grow more quickly then others. As a rule I inspect all Whippets' feet every two or three weeks and trim nails as required. An observant owner soon learns how best to keep nails well trimmed and neat-appearing in line with the structure of the individual Whippet's foot. In no case file into the quick with hand or electric file. A Whippet needs some nail to grip both in the show ring and for racing. It is abusive and inhumane to constantly cut or file into the quick of a nail just for the vanity of supposed beauty.

Always give yourself time before going to a show to allow your Whippet to relieve himself at home, and at the show before going into the ring. Many Whippets are excited on the day of a show, so you are going to have to establish some method of having your dog relieve himself. Almost every Whippet varies in habits, so allow time for the call of nature.

At the Shows

It is wise to arrive at the show at least one hour before judging. Be sure to place your Whippet in an area of comfortable temperature. If he is left in his crate in the car, *be sure he is not in the hot sun.* Don't ever leave the windows of the car completely closed in heat or cold. Dog show grounds vary greatly in comfort for dogs, so be sure your Whippet is comfortable before and after the judging.

When possible, get a look at the Whippet ring before judging. Show rings can be of all sizes, shapes and surfaces. If your judge is doing other breeds before Whippets, watch him judge a class, so that you have at least an idea of his style of going over dogs and movement patterns. The more familiar you are with ring conditions before entering the class the better able you will be to handle your Whippet to advantage.

In the Ring

Every judge has a different ring style. If your dog has outstanding conformation and movement, try, without being too obvious, to get as near the front of the line as possible. Some judges call the dogs to position in catalog order. In that case, there is little you can do to better your placement when entering the ring. If you have the choice, always get your dog between others of similar size. A very small or large Whippet can be at a great disadvantage if placed beside or between dogs of noticeably different sizes. If your Whippet has a good chance of winning, get just ahead or behind the dog that can give you the most competition. I believe in taking my best shot quickly against the best in a class when my dog is a well-trained, quality individual. If the dog is only average, I try to start off in the company of those less likely to win. Sometimes, the judge gets lost in his placements and you can have a good win by staying out of direct comparison with the tops in a class. A handler might as well learn to "steal a little when the opportunity arises" as the showing of Whippets in very large classes is highly competitive.

Always keep your eyes on your own Whippet in the ring. Don't stare at the judge, over handle, or constantly watch other handlers. Be conscious of their actions, but concentrate on your own dog. When the judge is not looking at or gaiting your dog, let the dog relax as much as possible, if he has serious faults, don't let them show, but do not tire him out with over handling before it is your turn for inspection by the judge. Just before the judge starts to go over your Whippet, have the dog in proper show stance so that he looks at his best. If your dog has certain qualities such as elegant length of neck and head, strong top line, good rear angulation, sound front, indicate gracefully with your hands these good points without being over obvious. If your Whippet toes out in front, has a ewe neck, narrow front, flat top line, cowhocks, or some other blemish get him in the best possible position to cover up these faults. Don't move the dog too much once he is in his best pose. Faults quickly become apparent to the judge when Whippets are not posed to minimize faults. Never try to show a judge the faults of a competitor's dog by using your dog. Always try to gracefully highlight your own Whippet's qualities at all times.

When asked to move your Whippet, follow the judge's instructions exactly. Learn to gait your Whippet at his best speed. Don't go to fast or too

The photos on this page show parts of the same class at the AWC West Coast Specialty of 1975. They graphically illustrate the need for the aspiring exhibitor to show the
best dogs he can in the best way he can if he hopes to come away a winner.

Bergman.

slow; gait at the walk or trot that shows your dog's movement best. Always keep the dog between you and the judge at all times. Do not string up a Whippet with a too-tight or short leash.

Most Whippets will hackney gait if shown on a too-tight leash so, when possible, have the dog moving freely on a loose leash. In approaching the judge after gaiting, allow room between your dog and the judge. Learn to stop your dog so that his legs are properly balanced under him with his head slightly up. If your Whippet has faults that make this impossible, get him in his best natural pose quickly with minimum effort. Many faults can be detected quickly when a dog is brought to a halt after being gaited for the judge.

After each dog in the class has been examined individually and gaited by the judge, the judge will often group his top choices together for final placement. Here it becomes a battle of handlers to show to the very best advantage the quality of each Whippet. If you are still near the front, as a rule, your dog is still in contention. If you are back in the line, do everything possible to show your dog's best qualities should the judge glance your way. At this point, you are probably not in contention, so do your best to gracefully catch the judge's eye. Judges sometimes reconsider, and you might get in the ribbons. If you are at the front of the line, keep your dog alert without overhandling. Emphasize his best qualities with your hands. Be aware of the judge, but do not stare at him. When you and your dog can relax and still fill the judge's eye with beauty and grace, your chances of winning take a giant step forward.

Many judges will have the dogs circle as a group when they first enter the ring and just before the final decision. Most want their Whippets moved at a reasonably fast trot, but some demand too much speed; a gait that cannot be executed gracefully in most cases. When asked to move in a circle, gait your dog at his most becoming speed. If you have a poorly handled, slow moving dog in front of you, pull up and allow space so that you can properly gait your dog without running up on the one in front. On rare occasions, in a large ring, you can go around such a dog, but don't be a speed hog. It should be remembered, the Whippet is a galloping and running sighthound, not a speed trotter. Walking and trotting gaits can give a reasonable idea of sound movement. Trying to assess sound movement from speed trotting creates confusion, and poor performance by many dogs, handlers and judges.

After the judge makes his decision, don't be over demonstrative if you win or sulk if you lose. Show your happiness by rewarding your Whippet with a pat or a tidbit. If he had shown well and loses, also reward him for his good performance. If he showed poorly, don't abuse him but don't reward him either.

Most Whippets quickly learn what is expected of them in the ring and endeavor to please. Proper communication and good coordination between dog and handler is an important part of assuring a successful show career.

If you have begun showing and are winning classes or taking points in about half of the shows where you compete, you are making progress. If you and your dog fail to place well up in the ribbons, it is time to evaluate your poor performance objectively. The two questions to ask yourself are "Does my Whippet have the proper conformation to compete successfully in the show ring?" and "Do I have the ability to handle to advantage?" It is not always easy to get an objective opinion of your dog from others. Show ring competition is the best barometer when you can't find the answer within yourself.

If you cannot handle well enough in show competition the services of a professional handler are a wise investment. Select a handler who brings out the best in your Whippet. If after a couple of shows, the handler does no better with your dog than you did, the dog's ring career should be discontinued, at least for the time being. Show wins are based on judges' personal opinions. When several judges do not place your dog in the ribbons or award low placing at best, you can be reasonably sure the dog is not a show specimen. At this point, consider purchasing a new, show quality prospect. You will have learned much the hard way in campaigning your first dog.

16

Selecting the Whippet as Your Breed

A NEW owner will not see the true value of this wonderfully outgoing, lovable breed unless both Whippet and owner can communicate on a basis of mutual respect and understanding. A Whippet devoted to his owner—and the owner showing the same respect for his Whippet—is an unbeatable combination. The Whippet is an ideal pet. He can be happy in an apartment, home or as a kennel dog. Almost all Whippets must be considered house dogs whether they are kept as pets, showdogs and/or for racing. Mr. Freeman Lloyd, in his book, *The Whippet and Race Dog*, published in 1894, makes mention of this fact. My work with the breed during the past 45 years clearly indicates the Whippet creates little or no problems under any type of normal housing conditions.

Appearance and Temperament

The Whippet is a small-to-medium-sized dog with males standing 19 to 22 inches and females 18 to 21 inches, measured at the highest point of the shoulder blades. At maturity most male Whippets weigh between 23 and 38 pounds and females from 18 to 26 pounds. The Whippet can be any color—fawn, red, black, blue, brindle, etc., and a combination of these

Everything about a Whippet suggests speed, even at rest or play. Here D. Jay Hyman's Ch. Highlight's Lucky Boy challenges his son to race—just for the fun of it.

colors with white. If you like flashy markings, the Whippet is your breed. The coat is short and easy to groom. A brush with medium to coarse bristles and a cloth with a rough finish is all that is needed to keep the coat looking at its glossy best. Naturally, there is little or no odor if the Whippet is kept clean. Generally with Whippets kept in the house, grooming every couple of days is sufficient.

Feeding is no great problem with Whippets, and certainly no other breed presents fewer health problems. It can be truthfully said that the Whippet has very few problems.

By nature the Whippet must be an individual and self-confident as he competes in races and shows as an individual—not as part of a pack or group. It is always unfortunate when a new owner receives his early education in Whippets from highly-opinionated people with little workable, objective knowledge of the breed. A thorough knowledge of the true development of the Whippet as a breed is imperative to better understanding the Whippet and his habits.

The Whippet has great eye appeal, with his streamlined outline, elegance and air of complete superiority. But the Whippet is not a snob and should never be treated as one. From puppyhood he inherits those traits of individual aloofness but functions best in the home as just another member of the family. Perhaps the major reason that the Whippet is not more popular as a very desirable pet is largely because many new owners feel intimidated by the aristocratic-appearing Whippet when he should be considered as an ideal pet. Do not be fooled by his aloof bearing. Treat him just as you would a puppy of any other breed, but allow him to retain his natural individuality. This, of course, does not mean he should be allowed to become a spoiled, destructive nuisance. The Whippet is determined by nature, but he fully respects a master that is also his friend and the boss when emergencies arise.

You, to a great extent, will determine your own success in Whippets. A close examination of the development of the breed through the years clearly indicates the Whippet is a true sporting hound, highly individualistic and competitive. Competition, based on the desire for chasing a moving object, is still a living, breathing part of most Whippets, regardless of pedigree. It would be well to consider whether you, yourself, are a competitive individual. If not, a tendency on your part toward curbing the Whippet's natural instincts would make for an unhappy owner dog relationship. It is usually the owner, not the dog, who bears the blame for the sulky, cringing, noncompetitive Whippets sometimes seen.

The Whippet is a well-established breed and cannot be changed easily in appearance or temperament. There are several types within the breed, but the Whippet can always be recognized as a Whippet. If you are willing to accept the versatile Whippet based on his merits and faults, you will find great pleasure in the breed. Some Whippet owners, ignorant of the

This lovely headstudy of one of Pat Dresser's Dress Circle Whippets shows the pensive side of the breed.

Always alert, the youngster has observed something that has taken his attention.

A Whippet family portrait from the Billings' Flyalong Kennels.

breed's background, attempt to downgrade his heritage as a race dog. This is a great mistake. It is the true racing inheritance that gives the Whippet his stability and courage as well as his elegant appearance and the great love of people that makes him a superior companion. It must be remembered that all Hound, Sporting and Working breeds were developed to perform certain duties in a superior manner. The purpose for which these dogs were bred should in no way destroy their value as pets and companions.

Reasons to Own a Whippet

When considering ownership of your first Whippet, here are the categories that should be considered:

1. Just want a friendly house pet (a Whippet or any friendly dog will fill the need).

2. Specifically like the appearance and temperament of the Whippet, who will be kept as a house pet, farm dog, etc. (eye appeal and friendly disposition).

3. Would like to show occasionally at local shows, fun matches, etc. (average soundness with limited major faults).

4. Would like to campaign heavily in dog shows (exceptional conformation, type and soundness.)

5. Would like to race with success (desire, alertness, balance and soundness giving appearance of strength with powerful drive and reach).

6. Would like combination race and show Whippet (all qualities covered in 4 and 5).

7. Would like for potential brood bitch or stud dog (qualities in 4, 5 and 6 with outstanding pedigree of producing individuals on both sides of the family).

Acquiring a Whippet

Once you have made up your mind as to the purpose of your first Whippet, then proceed to contact reliable Whippet breeders making your requirements perfectly clear and giving the specific reasons you want a Whippet. If you desire just a pet, the breeder should clearly explain why

The Whippet's agility is not reserved for the race track only.

An excellent hunter when given the chance, the Whippet uses keen eyesight to find his prey and his fabulous speed to capture it.

Pound for pound the Whippet is the world's fastest land animal. Only his courage and heart match his speed of foot.

Mains.

236

your new Whippet is of pet quality. Some owners who obtain their first Whippet strictly as a pet are often disappointed when their new addition fails at racing, showing or as a producer. This situation is generally the fault of the new owner, not the dog or the person selling it as a pet. Breeders, on the other hand, should be very careful in not overstating that a dog is of show quality. Many breeders of purebred dogs use the term, "show quality" entirely too loosely.

Your future in Whippets will usually depend on the success and fun you have with your first Whippet. Both you and your Whippet will find yourselves to be a combination of pupil and teacher, but remember all dogs are creatures of habit, so always teach or encourage good habits. When a Whippet learns bad habits, he repeats the bad just as he would the good. Fortunately or unfortunately, whether you start with a puppy or adult, the dog will have already formed some habits. Go slowly the first week to allow your Whippet to display his natural habits. Let him become familiar with his new surroundings whether he is a house or kennel dog. Do not pamper or reprimand too quickly until you know the new dog's already established habits.

When acquring a Whippet, be sure and get full information on previous training, habits, American Kennel Club registration papers, feeding, medical records and other necessary information. With some growing and older Whippets, the old saying of "you can lead a horse to water, but you can't make him drink," applies to those dogs who have already become set in their ways. Always analyze your own handling of the Whippet to be sure the fault lies with the dog, not you as the owner. More bumbling owners have spoiled a Whippet's temperament than have heredity and previous environmental factors.

The merits of a Whippet as a house dog are many. One fault of the breed is chewing. Chewing generally takes place when the Whippet is left alone in the house and becomes frustrated, bored and/or lonesome. When you are at home with the Whippet, he is generally not a chewer, but beware of locking him in a room alone. If a Whippet has great power for speed, he has equally as great power with his jaws in showing displeasure in confinement and being left alone. The wire crate in most cases is the answer to the chewing problem.

Don't be too critical in selecting your first Whippet, but be very realistic as to what you want. It must be remembered to find the perfect Whippet is virtually impossible, and to buy one even more so. Consider that your first Whippet should fill your heart with love and should fill your eyes and brain with beauty and pride, making you proud to own a Whippet. Your first Whippet is worth in dollars the pleasure you get from being his owner. Form a family relationship of love and trust, and the Whippet will be your breed for the rest of your life.

As elegant as he is, the Whippet can still clown. This talented trio consists of (from left) Moley Rat, CD, Ch. Meander Nicotine and Ch. Uruhu's Rolling Stone, CD. All are owned by Donna Bangs, Uruhu Whippets.

"Rabbit? . . . What rabbit? . . . I don't see any rabbit."

Epilogue

You HAVE read of the early and recent history of the Whippet in the United States. You have learned of the selfless fanciers and fine dogs that have brought the breed to its present state of perfection.

You have gotten a view of the Whippet in Great Britain and Canada and had a look into the world of the show ring, the race track and obedience competition. You have also seen how dogs are prepared for all three fields of competition. In this book the effort has also been made to show what a truly superior pet and house dog the Whippet can be.

The information on the Whippet Standard should give every reader a better idea of desirable type and conformation, regardless of the individual dog's intended use.

The gallery of photos presented here, some historic and some current, we hope brought pleasure to every reader. The Whippet is one of the most esthetically-pleasing of all breeds. His style, symmetry and overall balance have always been among his chief distinctions.

The author and the publisher both hope that reading *The Complete Whippet* has given you as much pleasure as preparing it gave us.

In closing the pages of *The Complete Whippet*, every effort has been made to touch on only the essentials that are important to those dedicated fanciers, both old and new to the breed. What might seem of great interest to one owner, might not have great appeal to another. The combination of all topics covered in print and picture will have value in helping you better understand and enjoy the truly versatile Whippet.

BIBLIOGRAPHY

ALL OWNERS of pure-bred dogs will benefit themselves and their dogs by enriching their knowledge of breeds and of canine care, training, breeding, psychology and other important aspects of dog management. The following list of books covers further reading recommended by judges, veterinarians, breeders, trainers and other authorities. Books may be obtained at the finer book stores and pet shops, or through Howell Book House Inc., publishers, New York.

Breed Books

AFGHAN HOUND, Complete	Miller & Gilbert
AIREDALE, New Complete	Edwards
ALASKAN MALAMUTE, Complete	Riddle & Seeley
BASSET HOUND, Complete	Braun
BEAGLE, Complete	Noted Authorities
BLOODHOUND, Complete	Brey & Reed
BORZOI, Complete	Groshans
BOXER, Complete	Denlinger
BRITTANY SPANIEL, Complete	Riddle
BULLDOG, New Complete	Hanes
BULL TERRIER, New Complete	Eberhard
CAIRN TERRIER, Complete	Marvin
CHESAPEAKE BAY RETRIEVER, Complete	Cherry
CHIHUAHUA, Complete	Noted Authorities
COCKER SPANIEL, New	Kraeuchi
COLLIE, Complete	Official Publication of the Collie Club of America
DACHSHUND, The New	Meistrell
DALMATIAN, The	Treen
DOBERMAN PINSCHER, New	Walker
ENGLISH SETTER, New Complete	Tuck, Howell & Graef
ENGLISH SPRINGER SPANIEL, New	Goodall & Gasow
FOX TERRIER, New Complete	Silvernail
GERMAN SHEPHERD DOG, Complete	Bennett
GERMAN SHORTHAIRED POINTER, New	Maxwell
GOLDEN RETRIEVER, Complete	Fischer
GREAT DANE, New Complete	Noted Authorities
GREAT DANE, The—Dogdom's Apollo	Draper
GREAT PYRENEES, Complete	Strang & Giffin
IRISH SETTER, New	Thompson
IRISH WOLFHOUND, Complete	Starbuck
KEESHOND, Complete	Peterson
LABRADOR RETRIEVER, Complete	Warwick
LHASA APSO, Complete	Herbel
MINIATURE SCHNAUZER, Complete	Eskrigge
NEWFOUNDLAND, New Complete	Chern
NORWEGIAN ELKHOUND, New Complete	Wallo
OLD ENGLISH SHEEPDOG, Complete	Mandeville
PEKINGESE, Quigley Book of	Quigley
PEMBROKE WELSH CORGI, Complete	Sargent & Harper
POMERANIAN, New Complete	Ricketts
POODLE, New Complete	Hopkins & Irick
POODLE CLIPPING AND GROOMING BOOK, Complete	Kalstone
PULI, Complete	Owen
SAMOYED, Complete	Ward
SCHIPPERKE, Official Book of	Root, Martin, Kent
SCOTTISH TERRIER, New Complete	Marvin
SHETLAND SHEEPDOG, The New	Riddle
SHIH TZU, The (English)	Dadds
SIBERIAN HUSKY, Complete	Demidoff
TERRIERS, The Book of All	Marvin
WEST HIGHLAND WHITE TERRIER, Complete	Marvin
WHIPPET, Complete	Pegram
YORKSHIRE TERRIER, Complete	Gordon & Bennett

Breeding

ART OF BREEDING BETTER DOGS, New	Orstott
BREEDING YOUR SHOW DOG, Joy of	Seranne
HOW TO BREED DOGS	Whitney
HOW PUPPIES ARE BORN	Prine
INHERITANCE OF COAT COLOR IN DOGS	Little

Care and Training

DOG OBEDIENCE, Complete Book of	Saunders
NOVICE, OPEN AND UTILITY COURSES	Saunders
DOG CARE AND TRAINING FOR BOYS AND GIRLS	Saunders
DOG NUTRITION, Collins Guide to	Collins
DOG TRAINING FOR KIDS	Benjamin
DOG TRAINING, Koehler Method of	Koehler
GO FIND! Training Your Dog to Track	Davis
GUARD DOG TRAINING, Koehler Method of	Koehler
OPEN OBEDIENCE FOR RING, HOME AND FIELD, Koehler Method of	Koehler
SPANIELS FOR SPORT (English)	Radcliffe
STONE GUIDE TO DOG GROOMING FOR ALL BREEDS	Stone
SUCCESSFUL DOG TRAINING, The Pearsall Guide to	Pearsall
TOY DOGS, Kalstone Guide to Grooming All	Kalstone
TRAINING THE RETRIEVER	Kersley
TRAINING YOUR DOG TO WIN OBEDIENCE TITLES,	Morsel
TRAIN YOUR OWN GUN DOG, How to	Goodall
UTILITY DOG TRAINING, Koehler Method of	Koehler
VETERINARY HANDBOOK, Dog Owner's Home	Carlson & Giffin

General

COMPLETE DOG BOOK, The	Official Publication of American Kennel Club
DISNEY ANIMALS, World of	Koehler
DOG IN ACTION, The	Lyon
DOG BEHAVIOR, New Knowledge of	Pfaffenberger
DOG JUDGE'S HANDBOOK	Tietjen
DOG JUDGING, Nicholas Guide to	Nicholas
DOG PEOPLE ARE CRAZY	Riddle
DOG PSYCHOLOGY	Whitney
DOG STANDARDS ILLUSTRATED	
DOGSTEPS, Illustrated Gait at a Glance	Elliott
ENCYCLOPEDIA OF DOGS, International	Dangerfield, Howell & Riddle
JUNIOR SHOWMANSHIP HANDBOOK	Brown & Mason
MY TIMES WITH DOGS	Fletcher
OUR PUPPY'S BABY BOOK (blue or pink)	
RICHES TO BITCHES	Shattuck
SUCCESSFUL DOG SHOWING, Forsyth Guide to	Forsyth
TRIM, GROOM AND SHOW YOUR DOG, How to	Saunders
WHY DOES YOUR DOG DO THAT?	Bergman
WILD DOGS in Life and Legend	Riddle
WORLD OF SLED DOGS, From Siberia to Sport Racing	Coppinger